The Cracker Queen

The Cracker Queen

A Memoir of a Jagged, Joyful Life

Lauretta Hannon

GOTHAM BOOKS

GOTHAM BOOKS
Published by Penguin Group (USA) Inc.
375 Hudson Street, New York, New York 10014, U.S.A.
Penguin Group (Canada), 90 Eglinton Avenue East, Suite 700, Toronto, Ontario
M4P 2Y3, Canada (a division of Pearson Penguin Canada Inc.) • Penguin Books Ltd,
80 Strand, London WC2R 0RL, England • Penguin Ireland, 25 St Stephen's Green,
Dublin 2, Ireland (a division of Penguin Books Ltd) • Penguin Group (Australia),
250 Camberwell Road, Camberwell, Victoria 3124, Australia (a division of Pearson
Australia Group Pty Ltd) • Penguin Books India Pvt Ltd, 11 Community Centre,
Panchsheel Park, New Delhi – 110 017, India • Penguin Group (NZ), 67 Apollo
Drive, Rosedale, North Shore 0632, New Zealand (a division of Pearson New Zea-
land Ltd) • Penguin Books (South Africa) (Pty) Ltd, 24 Sturdee Avenue, Rosebank,
Johannesburg 2196, South Africa

Penguin Books Ltd, Registered Offices:
80 Strand, London WC2R 0RL, England

Published by Gotham Books, a member of Penguin Group (USA) Inc.
First printing, April 2009

1   3   5   7   9   10   8   6   4   2

Gotham Books and the skyscraper logo are trademarks of
Penguin Group (USA) Inc.

LIBRARY OF CONGRESS CATALOGING-IN-PUBLICATION DATA
Hannon, Lauretta.
The cracker queen: a memoir of a jagged, joyful life / by Lauretta Hannon.
p. cm.
ISBN 978-1-592-40450-6 (hardcover)
1. Hannon, Lauretta. 2. Women—Southern States—Biography. 3. Women—
Southern States—History. 4. Southern States—Social conditions. I. Title.
HQ1438.S63H37 2009
305.48'96942092—dc22
[B]   2008049765

Printed in the United States of America

Set in Bembo • Designed by Elke Sigal

While the author has made every effort to provide accurate telephone numbers and
Internet addresses at the time of publication, neither the publisher nor the author
assumes any responsibility for errors, or for changes that occur after publication.
Further, the publisher does not have any control over and does not assume any responsibility for author or third-party Web sites or their content.

For Jazz Daddy & Princess Brown Eyes

.-.. --- ...- . / .. ... / .-.. --- .-. -.. / --- ..-. / .- .-.. .-.. .-.. .-.-.-

Contents

Part One
Comin' Up the Hard Way

Part Two
God Save the Queen (From Herself)

Part Three
The Way of the Cracker Queen

The Cracker Queen

Introduction

Everything You Need to Know I Learned Inside a Singlewide

> The art of living is more like wrestling than dancing. . . .
>
> —MARCUS AURELIUS

*G*ive me your broken and broke-down. Your worn-thin and your whacked-out. The undesirables, the uneducated, and the hopelessly out-of-date. For in them the human spirit reveals its strength and beauty.

I have been among them my whole life. I *am* them.

Our stories show that hardship and hard living are great enhancers. I'm sure that the pretty people have things to say too, but I prefer my pathos to come from somebody dressed in Kmart duds and missing a few front teeth. It just makes for a better story.

You, however, do not have to be toothless to enjoy this book. Just human. That's because we all have something in common: We know what it's like to be hurt deeply and emerge with a decision to make: What will I do with my pain? It is a question, one of *the* Questions, that each of us must ask.

Everyone wrestles with it, especially my colorful tribe of hellions, heroines, bad seeds, and renegades. But whatever happens, we never lose our sense of humor. And in so doing, we prove that the greatest humanity, and the loudest cackles, come from where you might least expect them: the wrong side of the tracks.

Well, even the bad part of town needs a good leader, right? That leader is inevitably a Cracker Queen, and you simply have to meet her. With one smack of her wand (which looks suspiciously like a baseball bat), she'll teach you how to live out loud, laugh hard, and love life to death. If you're smart, you'll want to be her.

This book takes you through my life and evolution as a Cracker Queen. My aim is simple: to make you laugh at my clumsy dances, to connect to you through my sorrowful songs, and to meet you on the path to Queenly Glory. Whether we get there or not will be determined by how we answer that Question: What will I do with my pain?

I don't know about you, but I intend to get there. Even if I have to scratch and claw and break a few rules along the way.

Let's start with a quick primer on Cracker Queens.

What Is a Cracker Queen?

The Cracker Queen is a strong, authentic Southern woman. She is the anti–Southern belle. She has a raucous sense of humor and can open up a can of whup-ass as needed. She holds her head, and her cigarette, up high. She cusses, laughs inappropriately, and raises t-total hell when the line is crossed. You might find her waiting tables or working the third shift at the factory. The Cracker Queen knows loss and hurt; these things have made her beautiful, resourceful and, above all, real.

Can I Still Be a Cracker Queen If I Don't Meet All the Qualifications?

Absolutely. Being a Cracker Queen is about having the spirit and attitude outlined above. Nonsmokers, Yankees, professors, and even men can be Cracker Queens. Your age, race, and country of origin are irrelevant. But your willingness to whup some ass is nonnegotiable.

The True Heroine of Dixie (And Everywhere Else)

Traditionally, Cracker Queens have been judged as uninteresting and unworthy of closer examination. The manipulative belle, on the other hand, has been the celebrated ideal of Southern womanhood. *What a crock!*

What really makes Cracker Queens notable is the perspective we've earned through generations of hard times. More than anyone else, we know how to find meaning in pain without ever sacrificing our trademark sense of humor. Adversity and a unique set of values have made us brim full of joy and able to laugh like a

Pez dispenser: with head reared back and mouth wide open.

In contrast, the belles bat their eyelashes and get what they want through false flattery and fake friendliness. Then they're miserable because they wanted the wrong things. We should have run Scarlett out of town on a rail a long time ago.

Anyhow, the Cracker Queen outlook on life is guaranteed to enrich yours. Of course it can get you in trouble, too. That's half the fun, because Cracker Queens can be both the life of the party and the reason the police have to be called.

When we make mistakes, we make big, messy, bodacious ones. The kind of conflagration that produces smoke visible from ten miles away. The sort that makes you cover your mouth and then secretly delight in recounting it to everyone you know.

As I lay forth the themes and tenets of the Way of the Cracker Queen, I hope you'll give 'em a whirl. When you do, you'll feel emboldened to be who you really are. And when that happens, the stars will finally come into alignment in bedazzling fashion. On that I'll bet my next five paychecks.

Read on. It is time to claim your crown.

Part One

Comin' Up the Hard Way

The Indian Princess

Mama was such a beautiful, dark-eyed child that she was known as the Indian Princess. Her young life was rough, and she remembers it all—being packed in a straw bed with two sisters and a brother in the dead winter all ill and bone-cold, the sudden sound of vomit hitting the slop jar. She recalls her brother Scooter ramming chicken shit down her throat and her Granny's surefire cure for pinkeye: "Squat and pee into your hands, now; then rub your eyes real good."

But what she remembers most is how she felt when her mama left.

It was getting dark that day, and the eight-year-old Indian Princess was scared. She had not seen Mama all afternoon, and her daddy, known to everyone as Bennie T, was a rare visitor to the tarpaper shack. She got her looks from him; he was half Creek Indian. But he looked strange—like a brown-skinned Welshman—all of five feet two.

When Bennie T did come round, he would stumble trying to pick up his little girl—leaving his smell of corn likker and Buttercup snuff all in her face. "You're my

S-I-P—Special Indian Princess," he would slur, making the words with stained, exaggerated lips.

Night fell on the porch, and there was still no sign of Mama. The kids started to panic, but the Indian Princess remained calm. As her sisters and brother wailed and huddled in the bed, she sat on the top porch step like a stoic. Somehow she already knew that her mama wasn't coming back and that the sadness would never leave.

Mama had escaped to Florida with a man who had an automobile and was nearly handsome. Nobody in the town of River Wall, Georgia, would see her again for eight years.

When it was barely light the next morning, the children walked the dirt roads to town. Their toes sank in the red Georgia clay—the kind that death masks are made of. The Indian Princess at last made her appearance in town, exhausted after carrying and half-dragging her younger sister the whole way.

On the courthouse square, the pear-shaped, busy-body women fell silent at the sight of the ragged girl. It was so quiet that you could hear a rat piss on cotton. But the men in town that day, mostly rangy farmers and chaw-chompin' sharecroppers, accurately predicted that they were looking at the girl who would become the most beautiful woman in Jarrellson County.

Jazz Daddy

The wind whistled through the cracks in the tarpaper shack on the day my mama was born. It fluttered the newspapers covering the walls and sounded like a symphony of kids blowing over the tops of Coca-Cola bottles. My aunts said it was a sure-enough sign of some kind, but every damn thing is a sign to country folks.

Two days earlier and worlds away, my twenty-year-old daddy was already a husband and already becoming a father. His time as a free-swingin' jazz cat was over, his path now bound with the briars of a wife and child. Gone were the easy days as a teenager in Pittsburgh, when his only concerns were the sound he got out of his alto saxophone and how good he looked while doing it.

Forty-five years later he recounted how a jook-joint woman paid him the ultimate compliment: "Boy, you're gooood. When I close my eyes and listen to you, I'd swear you were colored."

He despised musicians who hooted or honked or blasted their notes. His jazz jumped hot and high without descending into gimmick or harshness. His life, on the other hand, had turned hard and dissonant. He'd say of a certain flashy horn player, "He doesn't blow, he sucks." The same could be said of the situation he found himself in. Soon after his son's birth, the young GI had to return to duty in Europe.

Daddy experienced things in the war that would both shore up his Catholic faith and lead to deeper questioning. While in Bavaria, he met Therese Neumann, the Catholic mystic who suffered the stigmata on Fridays and didn't eat for forty years. Witnessing the bloody marks on her face and hands affirmed the beliefs he'd grown up with. But the stench of the Dachau concentration camp and what he saw inside would put him on a lifelong search for spiritual truths, often outside of conventional Christianity. I thought it was cool that my daddy had books on Hinduism, astral travel, the Dead Sea Scrolls, Buddhism, and UFOs. Everybody had a Holy Bible in his house, but we had the *Guide to Self-Realization Through Tantric Ecstasy.*

After twelve years of old-line parochial school and daily whippings by the nuns, he welcomed ideas that might rescue God from religion. And he needed something to explain the evil of the forty-two boxcars loaded with bodies outside the concentration camp and the thousands of walking dead for whom nothing could be done. Exactly 31,432 souls were liberated at Dachau, but Daddy's would never be entirely free again. They say it takes only twenty seconds of war to destroy a man. He was there two days.

Still, he was no tragic figure. After the war, he focused on his music, doing ragtag tours across the country in bands of patched-up men in patched-up cars, convoying from one questionable venue to another. The road suited him. When he wanted to think, it gave him long hours to do so, and when he didn't, it offered a ready supply of booze and gauge.

These extended periods of time away from home couldn't continue. His family was growing and his wife's mental illness and drinking were damaging the children. He finished college, played gigs on the side, and became an itinerant schoolteacher and band director. They had to move from one town to the next due to his wife's sexual activities with the men in town. Sometimes they left in the middle of the night, my father like a shamed troubadour without court or tights.

Occasionally I'll meet someone who remembers Daddy from that era. Grown women now in their fifties, sixties, and seventies light up when they describe his movie-star looks and musical talent. These women describe the same scene: how striking and exotic he was when he rolled into their small town, usually in a convertible with his sax case in the backseat. They never mention that he coasted in on fumes or that the car was crammed with five kids, a wife, and a basset hound named Dizzy Gillespie.

The man definitely had something special, even at the end of his life. I didn't realize it when I was growing up. Back then he was just an old fat guy with bad dentures who'd show up shirtless to pick me up from school. But we did laugh a lot.

He could be silly and great fun. As a high-school band director, he was known for his farcical halftime shows. One show went like this: After the band does several routine formations on the football field, the lead trombonist takes center stage and plays a solo—the absolutely worst-sounding solo of all time. Daddy becomes livid and grabs a gun stashed under the bleachers. A bunch of surly good ol' boys try to subdue him, but he breaks away and weaves onto the field like a madman. Then he takes aim and "shoots" the trombonist. Within seconds an ambulance arrives and attendants roll out the gurney. Stepping over the trombonist to get to the trombone, they strap it to the gurney and load it in the back. The soloist is left for "dead" on the field; the music is more important than the mortal.

Daddy staged that show when he was working in Cleveland, Georgia. After his stint there, he moved the family one last time, to River Wall, Georgia—home of the nineteen-year-old Indian Princess.

He blew into her town all right, but the wind didn't whistle and the shack didn't shake. The newspapers didn't flutter or flap a bit. But the aunts did notice a spiderweb in the doorway and a brown thrasher calling from the east. They were convinced it was an omen, and they knew exactly what it meant. They told Mama she'd better get ready because she was about to see the face of her one true love.

Four Roses

Some folks' parents meet while they're in college. Mine met in a moonshine stand in a pine forest—over an illegal sale of Four Roses Bourbon.

It was no accident that alcohol brought them together. Lord knows it became a central figure in their marriage before finally ripping them apart. But first they'd have a fine romance, the start of a deep, disorderly, and enduring love.

Mama was doing double duty on the night they met. She was babysitting her nephews and running her brother-in-law's home-based business: Skinny's Moonshine & Liquor. The singlewide trailer was hidden far back in the woods, so Mama could hear Daddy's car approaching for some time. She figured it was just one of her regulars: the town drunk, the deputy sheriff, or one of the pillars of the First Baptist Church.

When she answered the knock at the door, the cosmos sent a high-voltage message: A lightning bolt entered through the top of her head and shot straight out through the tips of her toes. She knew that the man facing her was The One foretold by the aunts.

It might have been love at first sight, but the second thing she saw was his wedding band. As she went to get the half-pint of bourbon stashed in the back of the TV console, she wondered who the stranger was and why he had to be married. One thing was for sure: He wasn't from around there because he talked like a Yankee—like how the people in the movies spoke.

The transaction was brief. He handed her three dollars and was on his way. As he walked back to his car, she peeked out the window and noticed he had a funny front license plate that said K4NGI. Then it hit her: he must be a revenuer—a government agent—Special Agent K4NGI! She panicked at the thought that she had just sold forbidden goods to a fed. She was still trembling when Skinny and his wife returned home. Skinny laughed and explained that the man was no agent; he was just the new music teacher in town.

From her job at the pants factory, Mama began to hear things about John Hannon. She learned that he had a wife with a wandering eye. That he was way older than he seemed. And that he lived in the big two-story house around the corner from Outlaw's 5 & 10.

The pants factory served as the electric grapevine of River Wall. As the workers sat side-by-side, they talked to make the dreary hours go faster. Gossip surged its way through the line. Secret truths, tall tales, and outright lies were uttered over every monotonous stitch.

Mama's cousin upped the amperage at the factory when he began an affair with Mrs. Hannon. He gave daily reports on his raunchy escapades. "I don't know what in the world you see in that old woman," Mama finally told him. "But I'll tell you somethin'; if I ever meet him on a dark street, he is mine." Two weeks later her cousin came to work with the news that Mrs. Hannon had left town and a divorce was under way.

Mama was hopeful. She needed something good to happen. At this point, the teenage dropout was already divorced and the mother of a little girl named Donna. She wanted to leave River Wall, a place that called itself "The Friendliest Town in Georgia" but was, in reality, so mean it was featured in an encyclopedia entry on the Ku Klux Klan.

Lightning bolts didn't signal my parents' next encounter. Sirens did. Mama and Donna were watching a movie downtown when they heard the wail of the first fire engine. By the time the third alarm was sounded, everyone walked out of the theater to see what the commotion was about. John Hannon's house was on fire.

Daddy was nearby in the pool hall when he got the news. Tearing out toward his house, he prayed that his children had gotten out in time. He raced past the crowds gathered on the sidewalks and toward the black clouds of smoke. Mama says she will never forget the look on his face. The house burned to the ground, but the kids were unharmed. What mattered had survived, but every trace of his old life was gone.

He moved his family into an apartment house where Mama lived with Donna. After noticing his morning habit of visiting the small rose garden by the house, Mama developed an instant interest in roses. She'd "just happen" to be in the garden when he was there, and they began having conversations about the roses. He adored roses and began to school her in every aspect of the flower. He also began to adore her.

Daddy wrote her a series of love letters addressed to Princess Brown Eyes and quoting Omar Khayyam's description of happiness as "a loaf of bread, a jug of wine, and thou." He performed Mozart's Fantasy No. 3 in D-minor on his upright piano for her. She said it was real pretty but did he know "Alley Cat" by Liberace? He played it perfectly, making goofy faces throughout. Love might have impaired some of his cognitive functions, but his musical sensibilities were intact.

A good job offer in Warner Robins, Georgia, eventually presented itself, and they all left River Wall: Mama, Daddy, Donna, and Daddy's three youngest children—the two older ones had already left home. Once more he loaded up the car and breezed into a new town. But this time he wasn't fleeing under the cover of darkness; he was sailing toward a new life. They set up house and got married. Daddy painted two red hearts on the wall inside the garage and bought two hundred rosebushes for the yard. After many years in the wilderness, Special Agent K4NGI was drinking the sweet wine of life again.

Bad Blood

ama passed a cotton field on the way to the abortionist and smiled. The field brought back the happy memory of being seven and picking cotton all night long under a bright full moon—the shiny white bolls glowed and sparkled, turning the field into a wonderland. For just a few seconds it comforted her, took her away from the desert of pain inside her. I know because I was inside her.

After five miscarriages, she couldn't bear to go through it again. Abortion was illegal, but she knew who to go to—everyone knew who to go to—an old black lady in the next county.

When she pulled up to the house, the lady was standing on the front porch as if expecting her. As Mama approached, the lady sized her up one end and down the other before looking her dead in the eye.

"Ma'am, I ain't takin' this baby," she said. "So, just keep your money."

Mama couldn't believe her ears and begged for help.

"No, ma'am. This child has a purpose in life. The

Lord says this baby's gonna be fine. Cain't take this one."

With that, she turned, went inside, and flipped off the porch light. Mama got back in her car and lit a Pall Mall. The nicotine took the edge off, but the dread was eating her alive. She knew something was wrong with the baby she was carrying. Her doctor soon confirmed her worries.

It turns out that she was trying to kill me even before she went to the abortionist. Her cells were destroying my red blood cells, the result of Rh incompatibility. If cancer cells are described as "angry" cells, I guess hers were really pissed off. In response to her attack, my blood seeped like poison into her bloodstream. The doctor said that we were battling each other, and as a result, both of us could die. They'd have to take me early, but they'd need to wait until the last possible moment if I were to survive.

When that moment did arrive, things did not go well. Severely jaundiced and anemic, I was still in trouble after two blood transfusions. Certain that death was imminent, the doctors wouldn't allow Mama to see me.

She finally raised so much hell that they brought me to her. They warned her not to get attached. If I lived, I'd be profoundly retarded. She told 'em they could believe that if they wanted to, but she knew better. I was still jaundiced when they brought me to her room. Daddy pronounced that I was the prettiest shade of yellow he'd ever seen, and both of them wept. When I finally got to go home, Mama carried me across the threshold as Daddy sang at the top of his lungs, *"There she is, Miss America! There she is, your ideal!"*

The doctor kept telling Mama that the retardation would become evident one day. He explained that I could appear normal for years until I got to the point where my brain would hit a brick wall, an unfortunate metaphor for sure. As I blew my first spit bubbles and gobbled my first solid food, his words droned in the back of her mind. But her fretting ended when she decided that the abortionist knew better than the men of medicine. Her words must have come from a higher source. Why else would that woman—a woman who had buried hundreds of babies behind the cotton field—save this child's life?

I have always thought that the way I came into the world—fighting and surrounded by fervent love—readied me for the bumpy childhood that followed. Likewise, the rough childhood prepared me to relish every day as an adult. Perhaps I'm proof that regardless of the hand you're dealt, great love can trump just about anything—even bad blood.

War Town

*L*ike doting grandparents, four nuclear missiles watched over me as I slept in my crib. They guarded everyone in Warner Robins, their pointy noses aimed at enemies who might threaten the town's Air Force base.

The world's deadliest military secrets and weapons were housed at Robins Air Force Base—you grew up hearing that, anyway. Scary stories about the base made up some of my earliest memories. When a friend swore that they stored nerve gas there, I figured that was why Mama always said her nerves were bad.

My babysitter described an area of the base where ten-story-high vats of radioactive liquids were stored.

"That stuff is so bad that just one drop of it could kill every living creature on the planet," she said.

"Even the bugs?" I asked.

"Oh, yeah, the cockroaches are the first to go."

I worried that the Killer Goo would creep out of its containers and roll like a thick, slow wave of glowing death into our house and neighborhood. The sight of a cockroach on its back would send me screamin', "MAMAAA!"

Over and over we heard that in the event of nuclear holocaust, the last place standing would be the base—the only survivors the residents of Warner Robins. The elected officials and other civic leaders said it with pride and a Pepsodent smile—before uttering the town's cryptic motto, "EDIMGIAFAD," a sort of cult-speak for Every Day in Middle Georgia Is Armed Forces Appreciation Day. The warning was that without the base, we had no reason to exist. No jobs. No future. We'd become a suburb of nothing. Like a cheap beach town without the beach. Indeed, there was no Warner Robins until the construction of the base made one necessary.

The vibe was clear and constant: War and weapons of terror equaled security and prosperity. You'd better be afraid and choose safety above all else. A feeling that things could blow and you must be prepared. It hung heavy in the air like a pregnant H-bomb. As a small kid, that frightened me instead of making me feel safe.

Then the UFOs came. Lots of them. The greatest wave ever reported, in fact. One hovered right over our house long enough for Mama to get us out of bed to see it. As we watched its red lights and zigzag movements, none of us felt like the UFO was malevolent; it seemed like a benign visitor—much gentler than the sonic booms farted out by the jet fighters from the base.

Daddy's cynicism about the military no doubt shaped my interpretation of the town. We had no connection to the base or to the community. No church. None of the things that moored one to a place. We were on the fringe—that's where Mama and Daddy were most at home. And in the first few years of my life, we were happy.

Despite the environment of EDIMGIAFAD, not everyone in town was a square. My hippie half brother ran the Purple Haze, a head shop that fronted as a coffee shop. Defiantly positioned right off the main drag, the Purple Haze served a clientele who looked like roadies for Lynyrd Skynyrd. Guys who wore their hair in single, waist-length braids and made pilgrimages to Macon to pay their respects at Duane Allman's grave.

Daddy was letting his hair get long too, and riding and wrecking Honda motorcycles. He was rarely wearing shirts when he was not at work. Shirts stifled him, made him hot, and he certainly wasn't going to wear one just because he was supposed to. He was old-school Bohemian and cared not one whit what people thought.

There was one item in his closet that he did enjoy: a black net tank top with a huge open weave, a rascal of a shirt—more air than fabric. It looked like someone took a long piece of yarn and crisscrossed it over his chest and gut, his white chest hairs poking through the holes. Daddy favored this tank top when he rode his motorcycle or took us on leisurely drives in his pink MG.

Mama was a rebel too. She wrote poetry and drove out to the middle of nowhere every week to take a poor black lady to the grocery store. More often than not, she paid for the groceries, too. In 1972 in Georgia, you just didn't see a white woman in a Cadillac driving a black woman around to do her errands. The Cadillac gave us the façade of respectability, but we had it only because Daddy won it in a poker game.

There was something literally in the air in Warner Robins. The jet fighters, the UFOs, an F-4 Tornado that decimated parts of town, and the birds. Fifty thousand in number, fifty-three different species. They were drawn to a powerful light in the night sky above the base. When the light moved down toward the ground, they followed and crashed into the pavement. The odd part was that the birds died of asphyxiation and were dead before they hit the ground. It was raining dead birds. The Macon, Georgia, newspaper showed a photo of the carnage with a caption that read, BIRDS, VICTIMS OF WEIRD ATMOSPHERIC CHANGES, LITTER ROBINS AIR FORCE BASE.[1]

Somewhere in the back of my young child mind, the atmosphere of Warner Robins made an impression on me, too: Question what you're told; don't follow the flock; living in fear is to be dead; and freedom matters far more than security.

It's funny that in this war town, with its nuclear missiles and Strangelove paranoia, I learned the opposite of what they taught us. That's because Mama and Daddy were my real teachers. From the pink MG to one of the first integrated Cadillacs in the county, the heart of their lesson was always the same: "To thine own self be true."

---

1 The Warner Robins paper never reported it, and the incident is not mentioned in the official history of the base.

Mama and the Chain Gang

*T*here wasn't much to do in Warner Robins in the early 1970s but ride around. So that's what Mama and I did.

During my preschool days, we tooled around in the butter-colored Cadillac, which was stocked with vodka and orange juice. I sat on the armrest in the front seat, biting at the air rushing from the vents. This was before child seats and air bags, but I had the ultimate protection: the Mama Arm of Steel. At the slightest tap of the brake, her arm would nail me against the seat.

Our greatest adventures involved chain gangs, crews of convicts working by the road. We never slipped anyone a shank in a homemade cake or provided a getaway car, but what we did do was just as thrilling.

When we'd happen upon these crews, we'd rush to the nearest convenience store and buy cartons of cigarettes for 'em. We might have been broke, but Mama was never cheap. She bought the best brands: Marlboros, Kents, and Winstons.

My job was to break up the cartons so that we could hurl the packs out the window. Timing was crucial, as the men had to snatch the cigarettes before the boss man, and his shotgun, could intervene. Not once did we ride by without doing something: Our mission was too important, and way too fun.

The excitement never faded. We didn't know when or where we'd come upon a chain gang, so it was always a surprise and a call to action—regardless of where we were going or what our plans might have been.

Mama would floor it once we were sure contact had been made. I'd leap over the front seat and press my face against the back window. I loved watching the prisoners smile and hoist the packs high above their heads as we fled in a cloud of red dust. Sometimes one of the men cried, but I knew he wasn't sad.

As a four-year-old, I saw the radical happiness I had caused. For the first time, I became aware of my own power—and it felt damn good.

I savored the view long into the distance. Once they were out of sight, I'd stretch across the backseat and picture them in my head—the men in stripes, with their wide grins and salty tears.

Discord

We searched every inch of the backyard for the gun. Mama had aimed it at Daddy the night before. Not surprising after everything that had happened. Being five years old, I probably wasn't the best searcher, but I was giddy like the others. It's not every day that you get to canvass your own yard for a loaded weapon.

Mama and Daddy were both drinking now, and the center of the marriage couldn't hold. Not after the "women" Mama brought into the bedroom, the kidnappings, and the affair with Daddy's boss. The worst part, though, were the fights, the knock-down drag-outs. They brawled behind closed doors, so the fights were an auditory experience, a sound track of horrors: yelling, furniture breaking, the thud of bodies slamming into walls and hitting the floor, grunts, and sick laughs.

I was so scared that Daddy was going to kill Mama. She had gotten banged up and smattered in bruises before, so I knew it was possible. I couldn't imagine anything more terrifying than not having her.

I'd try to be a big girl when a fight started, but the longer I tried not to cry, the more I felt like a big beach ball instead, my chest tight and bloating by the second. After a few minutes of holding it in, the pressure valve would blow and I'd become hysterical, shoulders heaving with sobs, snot running into my mouth and down my chin. My older half sisters, Donna and Cecilia, tried to calm me down, but they did a half-assed job being only twelve and fourteen themselves. When it was over I felt punctured, deflated, and normal-sized again.

Sometimes a fight would escalate so badly that Mama would gather us in Donna's room and barricade the door. Mama and the older girls blocked the door with a chest of drawers while I grabbed smaller objects to stack on top. Daddy would beat at the door, barking at her to come out. When the objects rattled and teetered, we knew the door was about to give way. We'd crawl out the window and run to the neighbor's house until Daddy left. A magazine poster in Donna's room showed a cartoon female figure with a giant black eye. A thought cloud above her head explained, I'D RATHER FIGHT THAN SWITCH.

Their love boat hit choppy waters when Daddy began playing lots of evening gigs and spending weekends on the golf course. Mama needed him at home; the pressures of running a family and household were getting to her, and she was lonely when he wasn't there at night. During those dark hours she discovered that Smirnoff and Pabst Blue Ribbon made her as light and happy as newly spun cotton candy. As he continued to ignore her, she set out to get his attention by any means necessary.

She started by bringing blondes, brunettes, and red-heads home with her. They had names like Zsa Zsa, Bardot, and Janelle and didn't come cheap. They weren't live women, mind you; they were pricey wigs. Mama was hoping to infuriate Daddy by blowing the month's grocery money on them. She placed the wigs on foam heads and displayed them in obnoxious places throughout the room: along the headboard, on his dresser, and by his tie rack. The creepy wig heads made the space look like a scene from *Rod Serling's Night Gallery*. Daddy was mad, but he was also determined that no woman would manipulate him like that.

When the wig spree didn't work, Mama noticed there were other men offering her all the attention she could want. A sleazebag named Bill would come sniffing around when Daddy was at work and call out Mama's name from the front porch. I remember that he constantly wetted his lips with a swollen, degenerate tongue. I didn't know what was going on, but I could tell by his oily mouth that he was a threat.

Another man we visited during the workday was Daddy's boss at one of the summer jobs he held. He had a son close in age to me, and they'd send us outside to play for what seemed like long periods of time. It's fair to say that this got Daddy's attention, but by then Mama's boozing was out of control, her sober self in tatters. One afternoon she warned him that she'd bust out the windshield of his Pontiac with her bare hands if he didn't cancel that night's gig at the Masonic Lodge. Of course he played the gig—and came home to a driveway carpeted in glistening shards of glass that crackled and crunched under his feet. Neighborhood kids came by to view the bloodied Pontiac for days.

Mama was coming unhinged more and more. On several occasions Daddy took me to my half brother's place for a respite. It was a blessed relief to get away, but I knew the cops would come and return me to her. They always did because she'd call and report that I'd been kidnapped.

The state sent a social worker to monitor our family life. This is when I learned to be charming. I had to. The stakes were too high. The social worker had the power to remove me from my home. As soon as she'd arrive, I'd bounce onto her lap and tell the story of the Three Little Pigs or Jack and the Beanstalk. Then I'd look adoringly at her and tell her she was pretty (she really was). And for my finale I sang:

> *"Jesus loves the little children*
> *All the children of the world—*
> *Red and yellow, black and white*
> *They're all precious in His sight—*
> *Jesus loves all the children of the world."*

Thank goodness she played along with the act and let me stay with my family. We might have been screwed up, but physical separation would have done me in.

My parents had most everything going against them

from the beginning. Their twenty-one-year age difference and the tensions inside their "blended" family put
tremendous stress on the relationship. But what assured
their mutual self-destruction were the wounds each
brought to the marriage. Daddy wouldn't acknowledge
that the hollow-eyed ghosts of Dachau were still following him, mocking his sunken dream of being a full-time
musician. Mama was still the mother-abandoned little
girl, the unloved Indian Princess, and would be for much
of her adult life. They should have tried to heal those
wounds before they wed. An abiding love and spiritual
affinity would not be enough.

When they drank to stave off the pain, they ended
up hurting each other physically and emotionally. They
hurt us, too, not realizing that they'd become the perpe-
trators of their suffering and ours.

As we searched for the gun in the backyard, Mama
said the neglected rosebushes needed a lot of work, a lot
of TLC. Fire ants had taken over the yard; their venom-
ous mounds were like land mines, and we were careful
to dodge them. The gun was never found. Daddy must
have retrieved it after the fight.

We were looking for something that wasn't there—
and running from what was. Just like Mama and Daddy.

Underwater Grace

My half sister Cecilia became a Jesus Freak in the 1970s. She joined a church called Bible Baptist Temple and even wore Jesus sandals. On her windowsill she kept a giant square-headed nail that she said was used to crucify Jesus. I couldn't believe that we had such a holy relic right there in our house. I was five when I began going to church with her.

The centerpiece of the church was a clear glass tank used for baptisms. I was dying to get into that tank. I'd imagine myself splashing and diving and turning flips—I'd be a miniature Esther Williams—pure underwater grace. It would be so fun.

It was a thrill just to watch the grown-ups going under. They were fully dressed—in polyester suits and ties, the women in long dresses. As they fell backward, the dresses would expand and billow out like parachutes—while the suits would contract and cling to the men's bodies—their ties floating to the surface like water moccasins.

I had to get inside the baptism pool. I had to. I memorized all the steps:

1. Walk up to the altar

2. Kneel at the feet of the preacher

3. Repent your sins

4. Accept Jesus into your heart (I loved him already)

Then you were saved and could get inside the tank.

All I had to do was come up with some sins. I thought long and hard until I had two good ones to work with. Now I was ready to get saved. I would declare my sins on Sunday and be on my way to my personal pool party with the Lord.

The big day arrived. The preacher issued the call from the altar. I put on a serious face and stepped outside of the pew—only to be snatched up by my sister.

"You can't go up there. Get back here!"

Sunday after Sunday I tried to tear away from her, but she managed to yank me back every time.

"Please let me go up there!"

"You can't—you're not old enough and you haven't even sinned."

"Yes I have. I have sins—big ones!"

"Shut up. You're embarrassing me."

By then I really did need to get in that pool. I needed to wash off the two big sins I'd been carrying around: I was a thief and a liar. I had stolen a nickel from my sister's piggy bank and lied about having seen the movie *Jaws*. It was eating me up inside. What had begun as a childish desire to play in the pool had percolated into adult-size guilt.

Soon afterward, the pressures of being a Jesus Freak got to be too much for my sister, and we stopped going to church. My sadness and guilt faded. She gave away her Jesus sandals. I buried the holy relic nail in the backyard. And although I didn't get baptized, we both felt that our burdens had finally been lifted.

Skateland

The visitor in the front yard stood eight feet tall and was covered from head to toe in pink fur. It was the night before Easter, and the Easter Bunny himself was in my yard, towering over a scraggly tree decorated with plastic eggs. I could have died of pastel-colored happiness right then and there.

My patience had paid off that night. When everyone thought I was asleep, I stood up on the bed on my tiptoes and peeped out the window. I gazed upon his glory for a good minute before he spotted me and—to my astonishment—he waved! I ducked down fast—I knew that I wasn't supposed to see him—it was just like the rules that applied to Santa.

I was already hyped about this Easter. Mama was dropping hints that I was going to have an unbelievable basket in the morning. The appearance of the Pink One confirmed that this would be the best Easter ever, and it was.

I awoke to find the living room sparkling with glittered candy and goodies wrapped in blue, yellow, and green cellophane. A huge chocolate bunny smiled from the center of my basket, and I promptly chomped his head off.

The big-ticket item was too big for the basket: a red tartan golf bag with a complete set of kiddie-size clubs. Daddy and I went outside to play golf. He had his bag, and I had mine. I felt like the most important little girl in the world. After each shot, I'd declare that I'd hit an Eagle, a Birdie, or a Bogie—he'd taught me those words already. Time with Daddy was a treat because he wasn't around much. He took me for rides on his motorcycle, and we flew kites once in the field in front of the VFW, but mostly he was away at work or playing gigs.

Mama had pulled out all the stops this Easter. She had a knack for doing things to the nth degree. Some thought her over-the-top style was tacky, but she was just a lavish soul with a funding problem.

Despite the darkness that visited upon her, she was a playful and affectionate mother. Every day she'd say, "I love you the most." And I'd reply, "No, I love you the most." When Daddy determined that I needed a whipping, she'd volunteer to give the spanking. Once the coast was clear, she'd close the bedroom door and whack the bed with a heavy belt. At the sound of each pretend blow, I'd let out a holler. When the "whipping" was over, she'd wink at me, and we'd walk out as if we were upset. I poked my lip out for extra effect.

She was also there for me when I announced my intention to join Donna and Cecilia in the twenty-four-hour Skate-a-Thon to Defeat Muscular Dystrophy. A preschooler in a skate-a-thon is a crazy idea, but Mama supported my dream. In the beginning I was wolf-wild with energy. I took the corners fast and did a saucy dance to "Louie, Louie" and "Hang on Sloopy," skate-song perennials. I got an extra boost when I won the Limbo Game, but as the shortest contestant by more than a foot, I was probably a shoo-in.

The euphoria couldn't last. After a few hours, I burned out and didn't think I could make it. Mama got me through it with her regimen of care during the brief breaks that were allowed. I'd coast over to her, and she'd peel off my socks, refresh my feet with a menthol spray, put on new socks, and foist a Baby Ruth into my hand. The other little kid in the skate-a-thon wore out early, plopped down in the middle of the rink, and wailed. Bless his heart, he didn't have the Mama Advantage.

I got so exhausted that I couldn't remember the end of the marathon. By all accounts I had turned into a catatonic on wheels—glassy-eyed, barely rolling. I received a trophy for being the youngest person to complete a Skate-a-Thon to Defeat Muscular Dystrophy. The trophy was treasured for many years. It reminded me that I could endure and survive. It was a talisman against giving up.

When things got tense at home, Donna, Cecilia, and I would skate our worries away at Skateland, an oak-floored rink near our house. At one point we were there seven nights a week. Donna, who was already a bad-ass, would terrorize anyone who even looked at me the wrong way. They knew she meant business because she had beaten up several older boys by then. A few of them had actually seen the bloody glasses of one boy who'd crossed her. Under the Supreme Authority of Mean-Girl Donna, we owned that rink. At Skateland I was carefree, protected, and could flit and prance with abandon.

There was one activity that brought the whole family together, and into rare harmony, and it was when we camped in the mountains. Something about being outside— outside of our house, outside of Warner Robins—suited all of us. No clocks, nothing to fight over. Just natural beauty, play, and ease.

We spent entire summers in the Great Smoky Mountains, where we built an impressive compound, pitching heavy cotton tents and shimmying up trees to hang swaths of tarp. Each morning the smells of coffee and bacon lured us out of our tent. Donna, Cecilia, and I slept on cots inside the tent, which had a moldy stink from the morning dew. The scent of mildew on cotton still makes my heart leap.

Mama's passion was fishing. She caught rainbow trout using canned corn as bait. Most of what we ate was fresh and cooked on an open fire. When the hour came for Daddy to start the fire though, the rest of us backed away to a safe distance and braced ourselves. The man had no fear or common sense around fire. We'd seen many an aerosol can explode in his face.

He'd begin by drenching the pit with gasoline. Next

he'd toss in a match, and—*ka-floom!*—flames shot up fifteen feet as he stood inches away, taking a drag off a Camel.
Our fears were well-founded, as he did start a small forest fire once by doing this. The park rangers were more
understanding about things like that back then.

During the day we'd take trips to see waterfalls and
dig for garnets on a mountainside known for its minerals
and gems. We went to Cherokee, North Carolina, where
Indians in magnificent headdress would pose for pictures
with you. The Head Indian scared me to death—he
looked like a mean version of that Indian who cried all
the time on TV about pollution.

On a visit to gorgeous Cades Cove, we counted
thirty-two deer in the woods and Mama said, "Now,
kids, this is really living!" She was always making pro-
nouncements about living.

The mountains seemed to look after us. Daddy
never set himself ablaze; the Indians were friendly; and
Mama, who couldn't swim, survived a sleepwalking epi-
sode that left her in the river. Childhood had its moments of pure joy. No more so than when we were in
the Smokies. But there were other good things as well:
among them the refuge of Skateland and an Easter that
could never be topped.

Addendum

As a grown-up I asked Mama about the Easter Bunny
in the front yard. She looked puzzled.

"Oh, come on, who was dressed in the pink bunny costume the night before Easter?"

"Retta, you must have been dreaming."

"I was wide awake. It was so vivid I could almost count his whiskers."

"You must have imagined it."

All these years I had assumed that one of Daddy's poker buddies was the Easter Bunny. He'd won the services of a one-legged housepainter and an alcoholic Santa Claus in poker matches, so there was a precedent. When the drunk Santa came to our house, he reeked of Old Spice and new gin, and I ran screaming from him. That Santa was real, but my Easter Bunny sighting must have been just one beautiful hallucination.

Goat Power

I was quite young when I first heard the Goat Man. You always heard him before you saw him. On the wind you'd hear the jingle-jangle of the goats' bells—it sounded like Santa's reindeer were coming. Then came the clanging of the pots, hubcaps, and scrap metal dangling from his creaky caravan. When he finally came into view, he more than lived up to his preappearance clatter.

Dressed in a torn suit coat and suspenders, he walked alongside the two dozen or so goats that pulled and pushed the caravan. Light flickered from his mouth when the sun hit his steel dentures just right. To top it off, his long silver beard matched that of Billy Blue Horns, his beloved, majestic lead goat. I'd never seen anything like either one of them.

The Goat Man traveled the Southeast like this for more than fifty years. The road was his home; his goats were his love. He was a gentle man, friendly to all who approached him. But he was filthy. He stunk to high heaven and cussed and preached at the same time. It was a big deal if he came through your town. Carloads of people would come to visit with him. Some brought home-cooked meals of fried chicken, potato salad, and pecan pie.

I got to see him several times, and the fascination never wore off. My mother worshiped him. If there had been a High Holy Church of the Goat Man, Mama would have been the head apostle. The minute we'd spot him, the sermon would commence, "See, that right there is a smart man," she'd say. "Material things don't mean diddly-squat to him. The Goat Man knows how to live—no bills, no worries—not a care in the world, you hear me?"

Not really. I was too busy wondering if he'd let me feed candy to the goats or drink their milk like he did, straight from a tin can placed under their bellies.

Not everyone looked kindly on the Goat Man. Some despised and ridiculed his lifestyle. One group of men slit the throats of eight of his goats and nearly beat him to death. Others stole a goat and tied her to the railroad tracks just before the morning train arrived. Billy Blue Horns was shot with an arrow, but he and the Goat Man kept on anyway.

Even old age and infirmity didn't ground him completely. When I was in high school, I saw him hitchhiking. He wore spiffy wingtips and walked with a cane. I blew him a kiss as I passed him on the road and never saw him again.

He's been gone a long time now. But something of him remains inside every kid who ever heard his bells in the wind. That something is a yearning—a clanging, bleating, jingling yearning—to simply be free.

Breakdown

*T*he kitchen caught fire on the day Mama had her nervous breakdown. No coincidence or surprise. Home life had been on the verge of combustion for a while.

Mama's sister Carrie was coming around a lot, and she was nothing but trouble. Whereas alcohol was Mama's poison, Crazy Aunt Carrie mixed and matched pills on top of her drink. Regardless of what went down the hatch, she ended up like a Redneck Vampire: violent and thirsty for victims.

Carrie and Mama had an unusual way of greeting each other. Instead of a hug or a hello, one would hold up a trembling hand to show how bad her nerves were. The other would do the same, and they'd compare their respective shakes. This ritual signaled that they were in need of a libation.

One night they hit the town so hard that at the end of the evening they couldn't find our house. They drove to what they thought was our street and saw an empty lot where the house should have been.

"Who in the hell moved my house?" Mama asked.

"I don't know, but I'll kill the goddamn chickenshit motherfucker that done it," Carrie vowed.

Convinced that her home had been stolen, Mama remembered that she had left me in it and she fell to pieces.

"They took my baby! Oh, God, I can live without my house but not without my baby! I have to get my baby back!"

They rushed to the police station to report a missing house and child. Dismayed that the cop didn't believe them, Carrie snapped and went for his gun. Mama got into the melee too, and they were thrown in a holding cell. When Daddy got the call from the jail, he decided to let them spend the night in the hoosegow and sober up.

He was getting no comfort at home. One Sunday he set up a chair and a TV in the front yard so that he could watch the Steelers game in peace. With a can of Milwaukee's Best in hand, he waved to everyone who drove by, just to infuriate Mama. Their marriage was circling the drain.

Mama hadn't been acting right for days when Cecilia accidentally started the grease fire. From the yard I watched smoke float above the roof and saw Cecilia crying in the doorway, fanning herself with the burnt oven mitt that she used to put out the flames. When I ran inside, Mama was slapping Cecilia and talking out of her head. Cecilia ordered me back outside.

I didn't understand what was happening other than

knowing it was real bad and that the woman in the house was not my mama. That woman was acting crazier than Ernest T. Bass from *The Andy Griffith Show,* and she had hit my sweet sister. That couldn't be my mama.

Frantic with fear, I raced my Big Wheel up and down the driveway. Would Mama ever come back? She always said that an invisible cord ran from her belly button to mine and that this connection was stronger than steel. Nothing could break the cord, she said. But I sure didn't feel the cord anymore.

Someone must have called Daddy at work because he arrived with my half brother and his wife in tow. They'd come to take Mama to a psychiatric hospital. When he approached, the woman in my mama's body kicked and screamed and put up a helluva fight. It took all three of them to stuff her into the Pontiac. They flanked her in the backseat, using their bodies to pin her down. All the while she was threatening to kill Daddy and cussing worse than Crazy Aunt Carrie. I stood by the scraggly tree and wept.

Mama was gone for what seemed like years. It was a ghost house without her. The life force had left the building. Daddy was now running things, with Donna and Cecilia doing the cooking and cleaning. I had not seen so much of Daddy before, and I discovered that he was OK—not the person I feared during their fights. Not the elusive figure from before. In fact, he was just like me. Although I missed Mama, I cleaved to him and found deep sanctuary. His older children called him

Papa, but Mama saw to it that I called him Daddy. I was becoming Daddy's girl, through and through.

Mama thrived during her monthlong stay at the nuthouse. She savored the rest and quickly became the leader on her floor. As the model patient, she had special privileges and was the only one who could leave the floor without an escort to get cigarettes. Her peers, especially the more psychotic ones, were a source of great amusement to her. She entertained us later with impressions and stories of their bizarre behaviors, as if she were just an undercover reporter there on assignment.

Arts and Crafts Hour was her favorite part of the day at the hospital. She made Daddy a large round leather key chain and embossed it with four roses, the symbol of their first meeting. He carried it until the day he died.

I was so happy when she called home each week because she sounded like herself again. My mama was back. Mrs. Babb, my second-grade teacher, was aghast when I matter-of-factly told her, "My mama had a nervous breakdown, but she'll be back before long." The look of pity was all over her face, and I did not like it.

Mama returned home with a prescription for Antabuse, a drug that makes you violently sick if you imbibe. I misunderstood and thought a sip of booze could be deadly. I stayed on pins and needles, afraid she'd sneak a drink and then I'd lose her for good. I worried that she'd have a nip while we were in the Cadillac and we'd end up wrapped around a telephone pole.

Her shrink advised her to do more for herself and

told her that she was doing too much for others. An odd thing to say to a woman whose selfish choices were causing strife for everyone around her. I suspect she conned him. She didn't stay on the Antabuse because she decided that drinking was something she did for herself. And after all, her head doctor did tell her to focus on that.

They explained to me that Mama had a disease: She was an alcoholic. As such, she couldn't control her impulse to drink. She was a sick person, a victim who couldn't help herself. Mama took this diagnosis and ran with it—drinking with self-righteous abandon. I've never believed that she was an alcoholic, just someone who enjoyed the bottle and refused to acknowledge its destructive effects.

Daddy and Cecilia moved out, and divorce papers were filed. A crushing sadness began to gnaw at us. We went through the motions of our daily routines like people do after the death of a loved one. Mama became numb and robotic. I lost interest in playing and cried whenever I saw the big-eyed puppy painting Aunt Carrie had in her living room. It was one of those 1970s sad-eyed puppies that had a giant tear on his cheek. When I saw him, I saw myself.

It was bad enough when Mama was away, but Daddy's departure and the collapse of the family wore us down to the nub. There were money problems too, and many suppers of dried beans and fried cornbread. A photo of me from this period shows a snaggletoothed girl with long, lusterless hair. I'm wearing a boy's shirt that advertises Honda motorcycles. I wore it because it was like having a piece of Daddy close by.

On the night Mama and Crazy Aunt Carrie thought the house had been moved, they both saw a vacant spot where the house should have been. It was more than a drunken delusion; it was a prophecy. A glimpse of what was coming.

Our homeplace would disappear. It looked the same on the outside but was empty inside, like a long-deserted movie set. Once you stepped in, it was all sawdust and dirt—and a few rags, bones, and bottles, remnants of the people who were once there.

Strawberry Dress

It was the prettiest thing I'd ever seen at Kmart, and Mama decided that I had to have it. The dress was red with white dots and had an apron and a broad bib embroidered with a single strawberry. With Valentine's Day around the corner, this would be my special outfit for the day. She went all out—buying shoes, knee socks, and barrettes to complete the ensemble. Mama knew I needed a boost, and the dress sure did the trick.

When I arrived at school that Valentine's Day, I was invincible. Mama had done my hair in elaborate pin curls, so I looked like a cross between a disco queen and a Botticelli baby. I smelled of Breck shampoo and Ivory soap. Mrs. Babb was delighted.

She asked me to deliver a note to another teacher. I unfolded the note before delivering it and saw that it said, "Isn't she the prettiest?" By the time I got down the hallway, I sauntered into that classroom like a runway model.

Daddy told me that we were taking a trip up North that summer, and the first thing I thought of was the dress: I'd have an opportunity to show it off to all his

Yankee relatives! I was elated—the trip meant time with Daddy, too. He had filed for custody of me but came up against a judge who always sided with the mother. As a result, I had only weekends with him.

Daddy and Cecilia lived in a $90-a-month apartment behind the M&T Drive-In, an X-rated emporium that showed celluloid classics such as *Little Girl, Big Tease* and *Help Me, I'm Possessed*. On-screen screams—of both horror and naughty pleasure—wafted in through the bathroom window. I'd run outside to where the screen could be seen through the trees. Whether it was blood-splattered cheerleaders or bell-bottomed swingers gettin' it on in a conversion van, those images mesmerized me.

When Daddy forbid me from looking, it became a deliciously secret act. I couldn't comprehend everything I saw, and it didn't help that the dialogue coming out of the car speakers was faint and garbled. But the screams, shotgun blasts, fiery car crashes, and moans were loud and clear. As I tried to understand it all, I cocked my head from left to right like a dog reacting to an unusual sound.

If Daddy was operating his ham radio, it was easy to steal away outside. Once he got on the air, he was completely absorbed in it. Like most amateur radio operators, his hobby was a nightly habit and obsession. His favorite way of communicating was by Morse code. The sounds of the code's dits and dahs were the background audio of my childhood. Crazy configurations of antennas and wires rose above every roof we ever lived under.

The best part of the weekend was sleeping in Daddy's bed—burrowing my head under his armpit and inhaling his scent of Irish Spring soap and tobacco. I slept with my arm stretched across his vast chest. He was solid—not about to give way, cave in, or otherwise fall apart.

In preparation for our trip north, I gave my favorite doll a haircut but botched the job. Butchered it, really, so she had to travel with a headscarf. Without it, she might have been mistaken for an early prototype for Bride of Chucky. My clothes, including the strawberry dress, were secured in a brown suitcase tied onto the MG's luggage rack.

The car was sure-enough pink, but it was supposed to have been Indian Rose, a hue my parents always described as "dusky mauve." Years earlier Daddy had wanted it painted Indian Rose in tribute to Mama. When it came out wrong, the paint shop didn't charge him, so he chose a free paint job over romance.

As we headed up to Washington, DC, I happily clutched my doll and played road games with Daddy. We went the whole way with the top down, my hair flying in all directions. When we stopped for gas, a guy looked at the girly pink sports car and asked, "Hey man, are you AC or DC? Or do you swing both ways like Tarzan?" I wondered what that meant. Daddy's nebulous explanation didn't clear it up, either. I was too young for talk about sexuality, and he wasn't going near it.

Ellie, my dad's sister, lived in Washington with her husband, Mel. Prior to becoming an academic, she had been a social worker. She lectured Daddy on the psychological dangers of allowing me to sleep with him. He shrugged her off and told me later that she suffered from something called Overeducation.

She had also studied Freud and noticed that snakes figured prominently in my play world. My snakes were dangerous and scary but ultimately manageable. I devised ways to keep them from harming me such as talking them into leaving. Other times I'd take charge and kill them by cooking them in a pot or letting them get close before I chopped their heads off with a butcher knife.

This visit to Aunt Ellie's introduced me to a world I'd never known existed. A place completely alien from my experience. Ellie and Mel weren't on edge about money; they ate fresh vegetables at dinner; and they had rituals such as cocktail hour but didn't turn into mean drunks!

Our stuff was different too. For example, the prized ashtray in our living room was made from a furry moose's hoof, while all of Ellie's ashtrays were dainty and made of crystal. Where Mama had a chipped Serenity Prayer plaque on the back of the toilet, Ellie had pretty Monet prints and Calgon bath salts in a decorative jar. I could have stayed in her bathroom for hours.

At home, my breakfast was coffee and sugar toast— white bread slathered in margarine and piled high with mounds of sugar and cinnamon. In contrast, Ellie and Mel each had half of a grapefruit, three-fourths cup of cereal, and a multivitamin that was placed in the cereal spoon. Sugar and milk were put out in little china crocks. Plastic never appeared at the table. This astounded me because everything in our kitchen was plastic. Poor people and plastic just go together. Ellie's place was orderly and calm but restrictive at times. I knew I couldn't sprawl across her white sofa with a bag of cheese puffs like I did at home.

From that summer forth Daddy and I made a yearly trip north. Immersion in this other way of living had a profound impact on me, especially as I grew older. The biggest influence on the person I'd become was my great-aunt Martha. I was only seven when we were introduced, but I thought she was somehow special.

I met her that first summer when we went on to Hartford, Connecticut, to see my grandmother Mamie and her sisters, my great-aunts Martha and Rose. The sisters had never married and still lived in the old family home. We sat in a dark parlor that was as cool and serene as a mausoleum. I could see Candy, their fat and happy cat, drinking from a Waterford bowl on the dining room table. Martha and Rose were cheerful and awfully nice. I liked my grandmother, too, although she seemed ancient, and Daddy kept shushing me around her and saying, "Not so loud—this could be the last time we see your grandmother." He ended up being right about that.

The strawberry dress received rave reviews in both Washington and Hartford. Even strangers fussed over me when I wore it. I hoped that I wouldn't grow so that I could wear it forever. For some reason I didn't put it in the suitcase for the ride back to Warner Robins. It was in the backseat instead. As we hummed down the interstate, the wind swept it up, and the apron started flapping like pterodactyl wings. The dress took flight, rising and diving, veering sideways like a stunt plane—until a Mack truck came into view and sucked it into its grill. My chin began to quiver. Afraid to tell Daddy about my carelessness yet desperate to save the dress, I finally told him what had happened as the truck was passing us. He was furious and told me to forget about it and not act like a crybaby.

Losing the dress was like losing the last piece of my armor. Watching it melt in the metal mouth of the eighteen-wheeler was worse than anything I'd seen on-screen at the M&T Drive-In. But the lowest of the lows would come next, when Mama moved us to her hometown of River Wall. Once again I'd find myself knee-deep in snakes, but this time I would not have a voice to woo them with, a pot to boil them in, or a butcher knife.

Wrongsville

*G*ranny's apartment felt like the inside of a tomb. A tomb anointed with Pine-Sol and talcum powder, the scents of old people wanting to die clean and smelling good. She was my great-grandmother, the woman who raised Mama after her own mother took off.

Everything about Granny was severe—her cleanliness, the lines on her face, even her kindness. When she was young, her father was ambushed on a bridge and murdered. In an act of Christian love, she sang a hymn at the killer's funeral. A more righteous woman never drew a breath. No wonder the air didn't dare stir inside her apartment.

We didn't live with Granny long, just until Mama made arrangements for us to move in with her brother Scooter. Not the best idea, but it was something. Mama was looking for the support of family during this rocky time. Trouble was, most of her family were A-Number-One Fuck-Ups, and Scooter led the pack.

Scooter was the nastiest waste of protoplasm that ever walked the earth. A real sumbitch. He preyed on children and served time for raping a retarded teenager.

Thief, liar, predator, and reader of the Bible: that was Uncle Scooter, and we were his boarders.

When his stepdaughter Misty took a bath, he'd slither into the bathroom and lock the door behind him. At bedtime he'd lead Misty and me in that creepiest of prayers, "If I should die before I wake/I pray the Lord my soul to take." Then he'd turn off the light and lurk over her side of the bed.

Mama eventually found us a house. The first time we drove up to it, I felt nothing but dread. The autumn light was grim and tinged with pure wickedness. The yard was barren. The house isolated, no neighbors to run to for help if something happened. The only thing missing was a sign that read THE BOOGEYMAN LIVES HERE.

The Cadillac died soon after we got there, and we were at the mercy of others for transportation. We couldn't walk anywhere because the house was in such a remote location. Mama was back at the pants factory and had to bum a ride to work every day. We wouldn't have a car for five more years.

Since moving to River Wall, Mama had been runnin' with a man everybody called Sock, so named because he never wore any. His identity as a friendly lush was so ingrained that it was part of his full nickname. When folks referred to him, they'd say Sock the Lovable Town Drunk. The town even made him parade marshal once to celebrate his place in the community. Like with Uncle Scooter, folks saw him as a harmless ne'er-do-well rather than someone whose actions were maiming a child.

Sock was generous, too, and left a hefty jug of moonshine on our front step as a housewarming gift. I dragged
it into the bushes, but the grown-ups found it and ad-
monished me for what I'd done.

From that first night on, Mama drank herself into
oblivion. Donna, who was almost sixteen, couldn't bear
it and left to live with Uncle Skinny and his family. I was
now completely alone and helpless.

Once Sock would arrive, Mama would put on some
mood music and banish me from the living room. She'd
later emerge in her underwear on the way to the bathroom. As she staggered by, she'd tell me over and over
to go to sleep. Sometimes I'd act like I was asleep just
so I didn't have to hear her repetitive yammering. On
nights like these I'd have to scavenge something from the
kitchen if I wanted to eat. I heated up a lot of canned beef
stew during the four months we were in River Wall.

Because of the distance from Warner Robins, Daddy
came for me every other weekend instead of each weekend. The time between visits was wider than all the
oceans laid end to end. Slower than tectonic plates.
Daddy must have been feeling guilty, because he'd take
me to the movies or buy me a small toy during those
weekends. He even stocked his apartment with Cracker
Jack—odd behavior for someone known as a legendary
skinflint.

I cried every Sunday when it was time to go back to
River Wall. Watching Daddy drive away in the Pontiac
made me think of a word Cecilia had taught me when

she was a Jesus Freak: "forsaken." Daddy looked away when I asked him why he was forsaking me. He said that certainly was a sophisticated word for an eight-year-old to be using.

One morning Donna came by and I lost it. Seeing her reminded me how much I missed her. My beach-ball chest burst, and I went hysterical—far worse than ever before. Yowling, sobbing, hyperventilating. She tried everything she could think of to calm me down, including the threat of taking me to the hospital. But what was in me had to come out. I couldn't stop it if I'd wanted to, and I didn't want to. I'd been walking on splinters ever since we moved there. Purging was necessary for survival. On some level I knew that and let it spew.

To be fair, the sun did come out once in River Wall. Warm, cheerful light for a change. It was a resplendent day. Mama stayed sober and gave me her full attention that entire day and night. We cracked pecans in front of the fireplace and played cards. She pushed me in the tire swing in the front yard. As I went higher, twisting and twirling, we both laughed—big, medicinal serotonin-explodin' laughs. This is the single good memory from that time.

Right before Christmas, Daddy came and got us both. We were moving back to Warner Robins, and we'd be living at his place in Driftwood Apartments. I was over the moon. Anything could be handled if Daddy was around, and my parents were acting like they were getting back together.

After the holiday we returned to River Wall to collect our things from the house. We couldn't believe our eyes. The place had been ransacked. Someone had broken in, stolen my toys, and destroyed Mama's potted plants. The blooms on the African violets were pinched off one by one. The other plants were uprooted and strewn across the floor. Those plants were near and dear to her, and the person or people who did it knew it.

In a moment of psychological genius, Mama said that maybe my toys were taken by somebody who couldn't afford to buy his own kids any Christmas presents. Maybe my toys brought happiness to a needy child somewhere. I liked the thought of that.

It didn't matter that the toys were gone, because I was getting my family back. As far I was concerned, the toys had been liberated from that wretched spook house too. To this day I hope that Mama's preposterous story was true. I know that some little girls never get out from the shadows. I pray that my dolls and my golf club set found their way to one of them.

Blue-Light Terror

*W*hen Mama and I went back-to-school clothes shopping at Kmart, there was everything: thrills, extreme danger, catfights, and con games.

Emotions ran high because we couldn't afford much, and Mama didn't have the credit card required to write a check at Kmart back then. If I was going to have school clothes, she'd have to hoodwink the cashier by using a fake credit card. And if caught, she risked criminal charges. She joked that with her luck they'd put her in the slammer and throw away the key. Based on our history, that seemed plausible.

Nevertheless, Mama turned the day into a major event. We'd walk around the entire store, making disparaging comments about things we didn't like and remarking on what we'd do with the big-ticket items that caught our fancy. Then we'd have lunch in the cafeteria—a splurge allowed just once a year because Mama said they should be shot for charging that much for a grilled cheese. We relished the grilled cheese like death row inmates eating the final meal. If she got nailed for presenting a bad credit card, we figured it would be her last good meal for a while. And mine, too, because Daddy didn't even have a stove.

It pained Mama that she couldn't buy me lots of things and upset me to see her sad about it. Complicating matters was the fact that I wanted lots of those things too. The tension between us was thicker than a drunkard's tongue.

Mama, who was slaving away in yet another factory, supplemented her income on the weekends by selling items she made. From cactus dishes to aprons, she offered variety and specialized in unusual items such as Elvis key chains and cats made from Michelob bottles and lightbulbs. Her people skills were amazing. As a result, folks gobbled up her wares. She could make everyone feel special, but she made me feel the most special.

Under different circumstances, Mama could have been CEO of something big. Her intelligence, charisma, and resourcefulness were a sight to behold. Until those occasions when she had more than two beers, she was a great mother. Drink made her mean and volatile, such a contrast to the lovely spirit inside.

After staying with Daddy for a few months, we got our own apartment only two doors down from his. I lost interest in the M&T Drive-In except when they showed *Walking Tall,* a movie about Sheriff Buford Pusser, a Southern lawman played by Joe Don Baker, who exacts revenge with a billy club. The movie had been released years before, but folks never tired of seeing Joe Don Baker and his hickory stick. I stood in the grove of trees behind our apartment and cheered on Sheriff Pusser at least a dozen times.

Then Daddy moved out of Driftwood and into a rental house. I guess he needed more distance from Mama. But we'd still go out together as a family, sometimes eat dinner together, and she even slept over at Daddy's from time to time, yet they couldn't live together. It was a confused arrangement and hard to explain to my friends or to myself.

The swimming pool was the center of summer life at the apartments. Despite swimming every day, I got pudgy from devouring a giant bag of barbecue chips after each session. The pool was my stage, and I acted out the elaborate Esther Williams–style routines that I had once fantasized about when trying to get in the baptismal tank at church. My audience was the sort that only Warner Robins could produce. A weird Air Force guy was always there. He told us to keep our eyes on the sky because when we saw black helicopters, it meant the nuclear war had started. Uh-oh. Nightmares about Killer Goo again. The guy was convincing and scared the bejesus out of me. He wore Air Force issue glasses so ugly that my hippie half brother Dennis called them "sterility glasses."

Being a base town, there were always foreign wives of servicemen around. They lounged at the pool too. Mama worked with some of these women at the factory, and they were typically abused by their husbands, either beaten or subjected to cruel jokes and games. Mama befriended them; she was a sucker for anyone who was hurting.

Her friends were usually Filipino or Korean. We never wanted for kimchee. Filipino Sam hung out at our apartment a lot. He had a Filipino buddy with him who had long black Farrah Fawcett hair. I thought he was dreamy. They spoke to each other in their language, and I began understanding what they were saying. They talked dirty but cleaned it up when they realized that I was on to them. Looking back, I suspect they were potheads, but I liked them because they were nice and laughed from morning until midnight. They drank heavily, but it mellowed them and I didn't mind.

Driftwood Apartments was the right name for the apartment complex. Its inhabitants were either adrift, washed up, or marooned—especially the people around the pool. On any given day you'd likely see a Korean woman sporting a black eye; an airman pointing ominously skyward; a Filipino Cheech and Chong; and me, a freckled preteen in a bikini, belly pooching out, hand in a bag of potato chips.

The pool was the site of my Tenth Birthday Party Disaster. Mama was half lit by the time the party started. When my friends' parents saw how inebriated she was, they yanked their kids back into their cars and drove away. I was wearing a new denim gaucho and vest set with silver stud accents, but nobody got to see me in it for long.

Just like that, the birthday party went poof. Mama was too sloshed to understand why the guests left. At least I got the Slip-n-Slide I wanted that year.

When Mama was too hungover to go to work, I had to call the shirt factory to tell them she'd be out sick. I hated lying for her more than anything. Many drunken nights she'd get on the phone and talk for hours, repeating herself to the poor person on the other end.

She'd call her mother, who was known as Me-Maw, and ask dozens of times, "Why did you leave me?" (Pause.) "Just tell me why you left? If you really loved me, you wouldn't have left." (Pause.) "Why did you do it, Mother? WHY? WHY? WHY? WHY? Why don't you love me?"

Slumped at the kitchen table with her hand on her forehead, these calls ended in a crying jag and an overflowing ashtray. I kept an eye on the ashtray for fear that she'd set the apartment on fire.

My nightly prayer during these years was simple: "God, please don't let Daddy die until I'm at least fourteen." I worried about him passing away, because he was older than Methuselah compared to everyone else's father. Fourteen seemed a suitably advanced age at which one could cope with anything.

One Saturday night I was at his house reading a Trixie Belden mystery, *The Mystery of the Uninvited Guest.* Suddenly there was banging and yelling at the door, and we saw it was Mama. She was far, far past the two-beer point. Daddy, not missing a beat, announced with a gesture befitting Sherlock Holmes, "Aha! We've just solved the mystery!"

Like him, I was an incessant reader. The greatest luxury of childhood was time spent among the stacks of the Warner Robins library, inhaling the unmistakable aroma of printed paper. If the essence of that smell could be distilled, I'd wear it as cologne and drizzle it on my grits in the morning. In fourth grade I fantasized about eating books and washing them down with a glass of aqua-blue plant food. When home life was bleak, I read even more, increasing the dosage of the medicine that kept me hopeful.

Against parental orders, I secretly read *Helter Skelter*, the account of the Manson murders and trials, and was jumpy for months afterward. The disembodied screams coming from the M&T didn't help.

A situation at my elementary school was also making me nervous. When Alex Haley's *Roots* aired on TV, the black girls came to the playground looking for revenge on the white girls. I was singled out because I refused to be a pushover. Anita Blecker was their leader. She looked at me like a cobra eyeing a bunny rabbit. She had been drawing blood since the first grade. Forget "see Dick and Jane." It was more like "Did you see Anita knock out Dick's baby teeth?"

Anita and her posse pushed and taunted us. They got in our faces and sang, *"You soda cracker, You b-u-t-t booty whacker."* Her breath reeked of grape Jolly Ranchers and pheromones.

Just as I was nose-to-nose with her and about to pee in my pants, Christy Smith materialized and saved me. Christy lived in the same housing project as Anita and had her respect. Christy was tall, thin, beautiful, light-skinned, and had the whitest teeth I'd ever seen. I don't know why she protected me, but she's the sole reason I survived elementary school. On the last day of each school year, Anita would promise to kick my cracker ass on the day we came back. I never slept the night before the new school year.

The thought of Anita only added to my anxiety during the shopping "spree" at Kmart. Mama and I argued over which clothes to get and which ones looked best. Go to any such store the weekend before school begins and you'll see this same scene being played out. When the mother reaches the end of her rope, she'll begin to grit her teeth and speak in a low, firm tone. Then the newly pubescent daughter will emit a shrill, high-octave sound. This will be answered by more guttural gritting by the mom. It's similar to a dominance ritual found in rams.

Our mutual edginess went into overdrive once the final clothes decisions were made. Mama said it was time to shit or get off the pot, meaning it was time to go to checkout. Awful scenarios zoomed through my head— Mama being hauled away in shackles and me being put in juvenile detention as an accomplice. Or placed in foster care by the state. The walk to the cash register felt like the Bataan Death March.

Calm down, we told ourselves. If the scam is to work, we'll have to act completely normal. We were damn good fakers. When the cashier rang up the clothes, Mama casually pulled out her checkbook and card. Still, the transaction never went smoothly.

First, the cashier turned on her flashing light and called for the manager. It took forever for him to come over, and all eyes were on us because we were holding up the line. I wanted to bolt but remained as composed as any other cold-blooded miscreant.

The manager would quiz Mama about the card, which was just a piece of laminated paper, a customer card from a mail-order company. She had her spiel down pat, but when I thought we were safe he would whisper something to the cashier. Oh, no, did he tell her to push the hidden panic button to summon the police?

But instead the cashier accepted Mama's check and returned the card to her. The bamboozle worked. It actually worked! With bags on each arm, I wanted to dance a jig right out the door.

Mama had risked it all for me. She was determined that I would not go without like she did as a girl. The Indian Princess got one over on the folks at Kmart once again. She'd live to see another grilled cheese. And I'd go back to school in the finest threads that a bogus credit card and an occasional bad check could buy.

Crazy Aunt Carrie

*C*razy Aunt Carrie is the kindest person you'll ever meet—when she's sober. So kind that she'd hop-scotch on gator heads to nurse a swamp-bound elderly person. But when she's drunk, the terror is enough to make even Osama bin Laden shiver.

Mama says her sister Carrie always felt unloved and unneeded—going back to the day their mother abandoned them. It explains why the sober Carrie buys groceries for poor families and takes in starving dogs. And it explains her fondness for mind-numbing pharmaceuticals and Smirnoff.

Carrie sought love through matrimony five times, but ended up shooting the first four husbands and going after the last one with a butcher knife.

"She just left his intestines on the kitchen floor—just layin' there," says Mama of the knife incident. "Good thing he's a paramedic by training."

I remember visiting the second husband in the base hospital after she put a .357 slug in his stomach. And Husband Number Four's name was Jesse James. She held the police in a ten-hour standoff after wounding Jesse.

He bled all over the shag carpet. Carrie must have had a bewitching effect on him, because like all the other husbands, Jesse James refused to press charges.

After her second marriage ended, she needed a place to stay. Mama was the only one who'd help her. Carrie promised not to drink or pop pills while she lived with us. I was eleven when she moved in and took over my fluffy pink bedroom with its posters of Leif Garrett and Charlie's Angels. I was now sharing a bathroom with a woman once jailed for assaulting a police dog. A woman who kept a fresh pair of underwear in her purse for those unplanned, yet inevitable, late-night liaisons.

It wasn't long before Carrie was hittin' the hooch again. Compared to her sister, Mama's drinking episodes were nonevents. After a few particularly harrowing nights, Mama asked her to leave. She left all right, only to return in the wee hours, crawling through the bedroom window and attacking Mama in her sleep.

The cheap diamond cocktail rings on her painted claws made a floral pattern across Mama's face. Tragically, she moved only a few apartments away and lingered like a low-grade fever.

Our phone rang off the hook. It was Carrie calling over and over, threatening suicide. She said she was lonelier than a peanut in a boxcar and just couldn't take it anymore. Mama got tired of hearing it and told her to just go ahead and do it.

Twice she staged hokey suicide attempts by shooting herself in the fleshy part of her thigh. Eventually Mama, and everyone else in the family, had to cut all ties with her. She became too dangerous to associate with.

I don't see Aunt Carrie anymore, but I hear she bought sacks of new clothes and toys for some kids whose house burned down on Christmas Eve. She gave them so much that she had to do without. I also heard she tried to run over Husband Number Five—repeatedly.

Some years ago she sent me a Christmas card and enclosed three Glamour Shots: Crazy Aunt Carrie in a fringed buckskin jacket; Crazy Aunt Carrie in leather biker gear; and Crazy Aunt Carrie in, of all things, virginal lace. She autographed the backs of them with her name in quotes: "Carrie."

She used to be real pretty, a dead ringer for a young Tammy Wynette. Now she's a skeleton. Mama says she always knew drugs and alcohol would kill Carrie, but she never thought it would *take* this long.

They say angels can take the most deceptive forms. If such creatures do exist, I hope they are like my crazy ol' aunt. I don't want the pale, winged kind you see depicted in books. No, my type of angel wears hot pink lipstick and totes a .357 Magnum. She gets her crown of glory teased up high every Wednesday at Myrtle's Classy Curl and Tan. And if you catch her during a rare moment of lucidity, she will do anything in the world for you.

Blue Christmas

*A*h, the Christmases of my youth. Family gatherings (Mama & me in our apartment by the train tracks); holiday treats (Cheez-Whiz and Little Debbie cakes); and gifts galore (thin, scratchy sweaters ordered through the mail, paid for by the week). But the spirit of the King was always present—not Christ the King—but our King, who died on the throne of a drug overdose but left us *Elvis' Christmas Album,* the holiday sound track of a million broken dreams.

After a boozy marathon of sad songs, Mama declared it time to put up the tree—an artificial one, of course: Poor folks can't afford a real tree each year. Like us, the tree was weary and missed the times when it served a real family. Our family.

The plastic pine had arthritis, her limbs twisted and stove up from eleven-and-a-half months of stillness. We smoothed and massaged her branches and dressed her in a skirt from the yellow-front dollar store. Now she was ready for her accessories.

For the most part, the ornaments are from earlier times as well: mangy garland; scrappy little Santa Clauses;

and blue balls, dozens of them, from when Mama overdid a blue-themed tree.

Next we put store-bought frost on the windows and silver icicles on the tree; when it is seventy-five degrees outside, you have to at least have the illusion of winter, even though in Georgia you might be wearing shorts and T-shirts on the twenty-fifth of December.

Since Christmas was not complete without the lovely aromas of the season, Mama sprayed a special air freshener around the living room as a final touch. The product was called "Money-House Blessing" and contained a magical Indian Spirit that would improve one's financial situation. Maybe it attracted money because it made your house smell like a Cherokee bordello. Anyhow, we never saw a windfall but used it every year, just in case.

We did have some newer ornaments made with our names on them. One said MAMA. Mine said RETTA. And the third one said MOHAMMED, for the Iranian man Mama married two weeks after seeing him across a crowded Laundromat.

I was so embarrassed by Mohammed. He had shoulder-length hair but was bald in the middle. His comb-over was longer than the tapeworm we saw in sixth-grade hygiene class. What was Mama thinking when she brought this foreign brown man into our apartment? He certainly wasn't my daddy. He was an intruder.

I quit the school play because I didn't want people to see him with my mother, especially in the school where

The Cracker Queen 71

my dad taught music. The problem resolved itself when he went to Iran for a visit and never came back. Stepdad Mohammed stayed around for just one Christmas, but we kept his ornament, just in case.

Mama carried a heap-full of hurt from being raised in a Holy Roller church that burned her Little Richard records. That's why our Christmas was devoid of spirituality and why she saw nothing wrong in giving vulgar gifts.

One year she gave ceramic beer mugs to her son-in-law and male friends. The mug was shaped like a woman's boob, and the drinker was supposed to "suckle" his Pabst Blue Ribbon through a hole in an anatomically detailed nipple. What's worse, these gifts were always a big hit. I never saw my sister Donna happier than when Mama gave her fifty rounds of illegal "splatter" bullets for her 9mm.

Except for the one year Mohammed was with us, Christmas Eve meant that Daddy came over to the apartment. As a born-again agnostic, the whole thing agitated him. He brought grumpy gifts thrown in a crumpled paper bag. Daddy railed against the commercialism of the holiday, which seemed only right, since he was the one who drove my tearful, silent Mama to see the loan officer each year, the patron of our annual celebration.

It took a long time for me to finally find joy in Christmas—it was synonymous with tension, debt, drunkenness, misery. But after a while I realized there was real hope in that purple can of Money-House Blessing Air Freshener. And love in the cheap sweater that took three months to pay off. And somewhere there was even faith—like a dim and intermittent light—faith that some higher power might just bring us a better New Year.

Ridin' High and Shirtless

*M*ama looked like a murderous zombie: eyes shot out from hours of drinking, knife hidden behind her back. Daddy couldn't see the knife as she moved toward him, but I could. It seemed to me that she was on a mission to take him down.

Half asleep and stretched out on the bed, he would have made an easy target. His arms were above his head like a baby's, and a radio rested by his ear. I crawled in beside him, clamping my arm and leg across his body and pretended to cuddle. Ten crates of dynamite couldn't have blasted me off of him.

Mama knew that she'd been foiled and turned to leave. That's when he got a glimpse of the knife and realized what I had done. He couldn't believe it, but you'll do anything for the person who is your everything. He was Alpha and Omega.

When I was eleven I decoupaged a photo of a bird for him on Father's Day. On the back I inscribed:

To me you're not a small, plain, crow,
But instead, you're a big, braun [sic] eagle.

He put it on display in his ham shack. All serious amateur radio operators have a shack where radio activities are conducted. Daddy's was a tiny, dark fire hazard filled to the gills with ham equipment. Frayed extension cords converged at the groaning electrical outlets. Their plugs were stacked on top of each other like leaning towers.

A window air conditioner kept the shack wonderfully icy—Daddy's cigarette habit kept it as smoky as film noir. It was the only room in the house with air-conditioning, and on sweltering nights he'd sleep in there on a cot from our camping days.

In this domain I was tutored in Morse code and music. As we listened to the saxophones of Cannonball Adderley and Zoot Sims, Daddy's delight never waned. Each time the needle touched the record it was as if he was hearing it for the first time. But he knew every note, every nuance. He also knew what he didn't like. We revered our musical gods and cursed the infidels such as Ornette Coleman and his free-jazz effluvial nonsense. We were not impressed with Stravinsky, either. "People are now seeing that he was no genius," Daddy said smugly. There was a lot of arrogance in the carcinogenic air of that shack.

André Previn was worshiped as a pianist and composer and Leonard Bernstein condemned for letting his ego eclipse the music. Mozart was The Man. A group like the Beatles didn't even warrant discussion. Anything abstract or avant-garde was deplored.

Once we were caught unaware when such a piece came on the car radio. The work was so absurd that I started giggling. Daddy quickly joined in. Each note became more nonsensical and ridiculous than the last, and we fell into such a prolonged laughing fit that he almost plowed the car into a ditch. Seeing that we missed the ditch by mere inches launched us back into hysterics. Tears gushed down our cheeks and we convulsed in laughter. We must have looked like lunatics to the people who drove by. They had a full view of us too: We were in an AMC Pacer, the classic glass-bubble car from the 1970s.

Daddy never said so, but I think music mattered so much to him that when it was done well he considered it divine communication. Its power surpassed that of the Hail Marys he'd grown up with and the Buddhist chants studied in later life. Gustav Holst's *The Planets,* a transcendent orchestral work, was our favorite mystical recording.

The Planets led us to long talks about religion, philosophy, art, and ethics. While in eighth grade, I became enamored of Hinduism, and Daddy found in me a fellow seeker. Lively debates about reincarnation and states of consciousness ensued. He challenged my belief in karma.

"Does that mean, for instance, that the thousands of people in the concentration camps died because of their karma?"

"Yes, it does."

He shook his head in disgust. I didn't know at that point he had been at Dachau.

The shack was also the site of our telepathic experiments. He was the "transmitter" and I was the "receiver." My sister Cecilia joined us one day and witnessed our talents. Daddy asked me to tell him Gustav Holst's birth and death years and I got them right. Next he asked me to describe an image of Holst that he was sending. Straightaway I saw a crazy scene of a man riding a bicycle in the desert. The picture was accurate—Daddy explained that Holst had attempted to bike across a desert and that was the "picture" he was transmitting. Cecilia was stunned.

Not everything about our relationship was paranormal or ethereal. In fact, he embarrassed me with the regularity of a metronome. Throughout the spring and fall he would arrive shirtless to pick me up from school. I'd have to remind myself that Old Man Winter would eventually come and force my Old Man to don a shirt. Cold weather never came soon enough.

When I complained about his facial hair, he grew a Vandyke to an exaggerated length and trimmed the bottom to a sharp point. He could have been a reject from a Rembrandt painting.

By this time his hair was solid white except for the yellow tobacco stains on the Vandyke. It pleased him to no end when I whined that he looked like the Goat Man. Heck, at least the Goat Man's dentures were intact; Daddy's were missing most of the teeth. When you're fourteen and your dad is shirtless, toothless, and telling Polack jokes, it's just not cool.

He had his issues too. In the old days he drank to mind-boggling excess and caroused with women other than his wife. He also had a way of cutting down his children with words. I inherited his ugly verbal skills and once made the mistake of sassing him in music class. He answered by slapping me in front of the other students. My cheek stung, but I resolved to get through the rest of the class. When Mama found out, she went on the warpath, informing him that it would be hell to pay if he ever touched her baby again. He apologized to me.

Before the Pacer he had a Volkswagen camper van. The seats in the van were set up so high that the driver towered over the steering wheel. As a result, when Daddy was shirtless in the van, it appeared that he was driving naked. Oh, the horror! The worst was when he arrived sans shirt to pick me up from marching band practice and the VW caught fire.

He jumped out and ran around the van like Benny Hill chasing a French maid. The engine flamed and sizzled. My hundred or so bandmates watched from the football field as he fanned the engine like it was a burnt pot roast just out of the oven.

I hung my head in shame and saw that the ingrown nails on both my big toes were bleeding spontaneously. It was the stigmata of being John Hannon's daughter.

We had good times and close calls in that vehicle. One summer we were camping in a remote area of the Outer Banks when an evacuation order was issued. A severe storm was approaching and everyone fled except for us. Daddy said they were overreacting, but I was a bundle of nerves. At bedtime he had three snorts of Evan Williams bourbon and fell into an impenetrable sleep.

Wind gusts began to rock the van back and forth. Sheets of rain crashed in through the window crevices. Well, I thought, at least we'll die together and he won't even know what hit him. I rode out the storm while Daddy snored the night away.

During that same trip he took a shortcut, and we ended up driving through a military base with live firing under way. We were literally caught in the crossfire, bullets zinging all around us. He stood on the gas pedal and then we ducked. Suddenly we were circled by MPs with guns drawn and pointed at Daddy's fool head. They questioned us and searched the van. One of them wore sterility glasses. I was embarrassed when he found the bourbon between the front seats.

Daddy and I made it through storms, gunfire, and an engine explosion in that van. It also took us to Disney World and on our annual treks up North. But the real action happened inside the ham shack. The music, the discussions, even the silly psychic games. Our relationship became richer and more meaningful as I got into my teens.

When Mama came after him with the knife that night, I was willing to sacrifice myself to protect him. It was the natural thing to do: He had been doing the same for me my whole life.

He was no small, plain crow. He was an eagle.

300 Minutes

*G*reat-Aunt Martha seemed perfect until the two-foot string of cheese got stuck to the tip of her nose at the Italian restaurant. The mozzarella trailed her animated head movements like a bad dance partner. What's worse—she was oblivious and continued to lead the table discussion. Lord knows it had already been a memorable meal; earlier a waiter had served a flambé that incinerated Daddy's neck hair.

Normally the sight of nose cheese would be hilarious, but because I adored Aunt Martha as an immortal, it was heartbreaking, irrefutable proof that she was human after all. Still, she was unlike any other human I'd known. She laughed freely and had a knack for making others feel important and alive. She lived with boundless verve and humor. An intellectual and a devout Catholic, but she hadn't an ounce of pretense or religious baggage.

Aunt Martha would have been a standout in any family. But against the backdrop of Mama's relatives, some of whom were literally only a generation removed from eating clay, Aunt Martha was a supernova. A cheeriness buzzed about her; she looked pretty in any color, any lighting. In contrast, Mama's kin were weary and sick, trapped in a world of polyester and pestilence and over-head fluorescent light. While hoping that their reward would await them in heaven, existence was grinding them down to nothing.

Aunt Martha, however, feasted on life and savored it like nothing I'd ever seen. She wore hats with plumes and grosgrain and spoke flawless Italian to the waiters at the restaurant. She traveled to Europe and quoted Chaucer at length. I wanted to be like her, but that was impossible because Kmart was not about to start selling feathered chapeaus; Italian was not going to be taught in my high school; and major travel for us meant going to the big city of Atlanta, for which Mama had to take a nerve pill. Aunt Martha had money and advantages; we had the troubles that come from being at the bottom of the heap.

We visited her each summer from the time I was seven to until I was sixteen. During the first few years all I knew was that I liked her a lot. It was obvious that Daddy, her nephew, was her favorite in the family. Always had been.

The visits themselves were not notable. We'd simply go over to her house for cocktail hour and then have a long dinner out. As I matured a bit, I found that being around her was like a Ferris wheel ride—exhilarating and nonthreatening yet giving me butterflies in my stomach. I'd never been in the company of someone with such charm and pizzazz.

Her magnificence didn't become fully apparent to me until I was around twelve. From that moment on I studied her every mannerism, move, habit, and taste. She ate hamburgers with a fork and knife. She wore a blue topaz ring that matched her eyes exactly. She attended Mass every day and imbibed two stiff Old-Fashioneds before supper. I thought about imitating her, but it felt pointless since she was out of my league.

Quite gradually I realized that what made Aunt Martha captivating was not the fancy hats and trips or topaz ring—it was her love of life and the loving way she responded to every person and situation, as if in a state of perpetual gladness. Then came the epiphany: I can be like her because I have a choice in how I see and react to things. I can choose to accept whatever comes at me with love and gratitude. I don't have to be oppressed— or anybody's victim. I can live large even if I'm huddling in a hovel.

It was a staggering notion. When you're raised in an environment of people holding themselves and each other down, it has an insidious influence on your think- ing, your expectations, and your choices. It can taint your mind to the point of actually becoming a form of mental illness.

You either dream measly dreams or far-fetched ones such as what you'll do if you win the lottery. You live on the defense, waiting for the disappointment to re- veal itself and for everything to fold. Menacing voices roost in your brain, ready to steer you in the wrong direction when a life-changing opportunity comes. They chant, *"You can't do that. You're not good enough. You won't succeed."*

When I shifted into Aunt Martha's way of receiving the world, my world got brighter and the voices weaker. At fifteen I was coming into my own. I started wearing red lipstick and drinking Dr Pepper from a wineglass. Most importantly, I began writing—the activity that has brought me closer to God than anything else.

Each summer I spent an average of five hours with Aunt Martha. It's a marvel that being in her company for just three hundred minutes brought about a self-awakening that is still unfolding.

After I graduated from high school, we maintained a lively correspondence until Alzheimer's made her a child again. She always closed her letters with a remark about the beauty of New England at that time of year, whatever that time of year happened to be. As a final flourish, she'd give a bit of advice such as "Keep the flags of life flying!" or "Use your good head at all times!" In the latter she underlined each word for enthusiastic emphasis.

"Life is a banquet, and most poor suckers are starving to death," said that other, more famous aunt, Auntie Mame. Most of us are starving because we don't even believe the banquet exists—or that it's accessible to people like us. My great-aunt Martha not only showed me the banquet, she pointed the way to abundance itself.

Fortune Presents Gifts Not According to the Book

December 30, 1985

"I want you to know that I've reached bodhisattva.[1] I have settled everything in my life and am at peace."

As my father spoke those words it was as if he was looking past me and extracting my bone marrow at the same time. I never wanted to see or feel that look in his eye again.

He had been ill with a cold or flu for two weeks and decided that day to stop smoking. There was a lot wrong with this picture. He rarely got sick, and when he did it didn't linger for more than a few days. Never before had he wanted to tell me about the state of his soul, as if preparing me for something only he knew was going to happen. And why, after fifty years of nicotine addiction, did he now decide to give it up? My gut hinted at the answer, but I dismissed it.

---

1 A state of enlightenment in which the being compassionately refrains from entering nirvana in order to help liberate others.

I was seventeen and preoccupied with a more pressing matter: what I was going to wear when I went out on New Year's Eve. My friend David had scoped out a club that would gladly serve underage drinkers, so foremost on my mind was assembling the right party outfit. I settled on an oversized teal jacket with 1980s shoulder pads the size of a linebacker's. My best friend Rachel had made it, and it was my favorite piece of clothing. I wore it with trousers and flapper-length pearls that nearly touched my knees. When I modeled the ensemble for Daddy, he roared and asked if I was serious. I assured him I was. After he said it looked like a zoot suit, I twirled my plastic pearls and stomped off.

January 1, 1986

David and I danced and drank the night away. He drove me home around four a.m., and we sat in the car talking about whether we should play with the Ouija board. As I reached for the board, we were scared out of our wits by a figure stumbling and weaving toward the car. It was my soused mama, returning home from Daddy's. Suspicious behavior: she was dating someone and estranged from Daddy.

Once she was safely inside the house, we set up the Ouija board in the car. As it has done to teenagers since time immemorial, it proceeded to freak us out. The planchette flew violently—repeatedly spelling DEAD DADDY . . . DEAD DADDY . . . DEAD DADDY.

We asked how and when this Daddy was going to

die and it responded, TODAY . . . HEART ATTACK . . . TODAY
HEART ATTACK . . . TODAYTODAYTODAY.

The bone-marrow feeling came back, and I ended
the game. "Just a mischievous spirit," I said. "I'm going
to bed."

Later on January 1, 1986

I am jolted awake by Daddy yelling for me. He is doubled
over at the kitchen counter, ordering me to call an ambulance. As soon as I finished the call, I ran to hug him,
but he knocked me away with a power I can describe
only as otherworldly. I got back on the phone and called
Mama and my sister Cecilia, but no one answered.

The ambulance men arrived and made him sit down.
His blood pressure was 45/20, and they inserted tubes
and put an oxygen mask in place. Daddy asked, "May I
expectorate?" The EMT didn't understand, so Daddy
tried again, this time more desperate, "Can I spit?!"

I rode in the front seat of the ambulance, which appeared to take the scenic route, inching along at what
seemed like five miles per hour. People gawked at us all
along the way, and I hated them for it.

Finally at the hospital, I went straight to the chapel
so that I could be in a quiet, solitary place. Mama found
out about everything and went to be with Daddy.

In the chapel I prayed hard—not asking for his life
to be spared, but for strength for all of us to cope with
whatever the outcome. I thought intercessionary prayer
was a waste of time because the laws of the Universe

were fixed. Karmic debts could not be changed. Then the most stunning thing struck me physically—a surging electrical current entered the top center of my head and coursed through my body. It was a full-force calmness. It was Daddy saying, "I'm finished. ALL IS WELL."

A lightning bolt hit Mama when she first met Daddy in the moonshine trailer, and he left me with the same sensation. For someone who detested melodrama, he sure had a knack for flashy entrances and exits.

Five minutes later Mama and a nurse named Cher entered the chapel. "You don't have to say anything," I said. "I know he's gone."

The grief and hurt were cataclysmic, but the calmness stayed with me. It sounds odd, but even as I stood in the chapel, I felt thankful. As a girl I'd prayed for him to stay alive until I was at least fourteen, and I was fully aware that I'd gotten three bonus years beyond what I'd bargained for. All along I knew that our time together was brittle and that he'd die before my adulthood. He was sixty-two.

Fearing that his death would set us dangerously back, I continued to pray that we'd somehow learn from it and move forward. If I didn't use my good head, I'd end up under the train or down the well—or in any such place without windows or doors, let alone feasts or banquets.

Nurse Cher then handed me a Valium that I carried in my wallet for six months. I never took it because I figured that I needed to experience the pain honestly and not cover it up. But I wasn't sure how long I could sustain that much honest pain, so I kept the pill handy.

Believing as I did in reincarnation, I had the saddest thought: What if he was being born again in some other hospital—letting out a birth cry and starting over? But I recalled what he said about attaining bodhisattva, and it comforted me, even if I might have been skeptical about his self-assessment.

The nightmares began that first night and came after me every night for four months. Back-to-back dreams of Daddy dying of every conceivable cause and in every sort of scenario. Cancer, car accident, electrocution, falling down a staircase, murder, drowning, fire, hanging, hit-and-run, Lou Gehrig's disease, bullet to the head, snared in an animal trap, vampire attack, hypothermia, asphyxiation, radiation—every manner but the one that did kill him: a heart attack. A dozen nightmares in a row, each remembered in vivid detail upon waking.

The Morse code started that first night, too. Loud and persistent—and lasting an hour or more—the dits and dahs wafted into our house for several days after he died. Too terrified to decipher it, I tried to tune it out instead. It had to be an auditory hallucination anyway, I told myself, not a ghostly transmission. We were accustomed to hearing Morse code blaring from his double-wide two doors down, and I was sure that my mind was just playing tricks on me. Somehow Cecilia heard it miles away at her house too.

I returned to school and was treated like a leper at first. Friends averted their eyes as if to ward off the Maiden of

Death herself. Teachers gave me the same look as Mrs. Babb when I told her in the second grade about Mama's nervous breakdown. For her part, Mama didn't take a sip of alcohol for months.

I posted a Sanskrit saying in my locker:

Deep in the sea are riches beyond compare,
But if you seek safety, it is on the shore.

Determined to get off the shore, I made plans to graduate early from high school and work and save money so that I could go to Europe on my own. I focused on living instead of withering. Risking rather than fearing, even though I was afraid. I ached, but I also felt lucky to have had Daddy in my life. Incredibly lucky.

Don't think for a minute that I was some youthful Buddha with a penchant for suffering. I was cracked and throbbing—and as clueless as anyone else my age. The difference was that I knew how easily and permanently I could break, so I had to be diligent.

His absence was present always, like an invisible little brat demanding attention. He followed my every move—popping my waistband when I wasn't looking, yanking my braid, sitting by me on the bed but never going to sleep. It was so palpable that I'm surprised I didn't start talking out loud to him. His behavior finally improved when I quit trying to outrun him.

Daddy's death showed on Mama's face as if she were wearing foundation four shades too light. I attributed it to a bad choice of makeup. But in retrospect, it was shell shock and unvarnished sorrow. Regret over unfinished business with a man who came into her life bearing a mixed platter, the meat half-rotten but delectable and ringed in diamonds.

Daddy was buried at the national cemetery in Andersonville, Georgia. The site was originally a notorious Civil War POW camp where thousands of Yankee soldiers perished. He enjoyed the irony of one day being interred with his compatriots. No matter how long he lived in the South, he was always an outsider.

Aunt Ellie fretted over his fallen Catholic soul until she received a letter from a nun who had known them as children. The nun told her not to worry. She explained that anyone who loved music as he did was undoubtedly, unequivocally in heaven. For his sake I hoped Stravinsky was not in the conductor's chair.

The gifts my father gave me are many. In life, he was my lifeline. In death he taught me that everything must end and that it's OK. That time is short and you'd better do what you can with now. And because anything can be gone in a flash, we'd better love one another. We hear this ad nauseam, but there's a reason it still stands. To understand it at the age of seventeen is both a tragedy and a boon.

Daddy died practically penniless and left me with nothing. Nothing but these priceless gifts.

Part Two

God Save the Queen
(From Herself)

**All the world's a stage
and most of us are desperately unrehearsed.**

—Seán O'Casey

The Tree That Owns Itself

*A*s it turns out, I did make it to Europe and enrolled at the University of Georgia (UGA) when I returned. I'd been accepted to the school several months before Daddy died. It was always assumed that I'd go to college, as I was an eager student and chronic over-achiever. But I had not even visited the campus before I loaded up Mama's car and drove myself to the dorm.

With the help of federal grants and loans, a scholarship, and assistance from Aunt Ellie, I made it through my freshman year. That spring arrived like a ravishing prostitute, abloom in profuse color and lush perfume. Daffodils, wisteria, gardenias, kudzu, and magnolias burst forth and stayed forth for an unnaturally long period. Their fragrances mingled and gained strength under the tree canopies throughout town. You couldn't ride your bike thirty feet without getting a vine in your spokes.

The college town had become a shady, undulating jungle Eden. It triggered something in me that April, and I went hog wild. Away from the confines of Warner Robins, I took full advantage of the bohemian mecca that was Athens, Georgia.

I skipped algebra and dropped acid. I wrote some of the worst verse in the history of words. My makeup imitated Cyndi Lauper and Boy George, and looking back at it, made me resemble an alarmed drag queen. I was living carefree and flamboyantly and putting into practice those gifts my father had given me—or at least my interpretation of them.

There's a famous oak tree in Athens called the Tree That Owns Itself. Like the oak, I too was becoming more self-possessed. After a young lifetime of being responsible and mature in the face of difficulties, I had cut loose and was having fun. I tried to bring along as many people as I could on my joy ride.

Once I'd smoked pot a few times, I decided that everyone on my dorm hall needed to be initiated into that enjoyment. Those girls, especially the uptight ones who had never disobeyed or questioned anyone or anything in their lives, couldn't get enough of the Mother Herb. My room, which I'd already christened the Opium Den, was the official marijuana training facility for the ninth floor of Brumby Hall. I instructed my students in All Things Weed—from how to fashion a bong out of a Coke can to how to select incense to mask that telltale smell. I delighted in their progress and celebrated our mutual debauchery.

To be honest, I was never much of a druggie, just interested in experimenting. Since I was always mindful that time was short, I didn't want to be drunk or high at some critical life moment. In fact, I was a disappointing prude compared to the hardcore hooligans in my orbit.

Poems, music, and art were the name of my game. They were my dope. I dropped out of the university in my sophomore year to "court the muse" and my apartment became something of a salon for artists and musicians. I wrote furiously in my journals, held poetry readings, and was a guest flautist in several bands. I was also barely scraping by.

One afternoon I stood in the Salvation Army soup line for two hours alongside gutter bums and muttering psychos before being turned away at the door. They said they needed documentation that I was poor. Why else would I wait two hours for spaghetti noodles and a stale doughnut?!

Mama did the best she could in sending money from time to time, and I had a part-time clerical job on campus, but cash flow remained elusive. Eventually realizing that I didn't want to be a broke beatnik at age forty, I reenrolled at the university and found my groove—still living creatively but motivated to complete my studies. Then another lightning bolt—this time when I laid eyes on a guy named Jim. He owned a record store downtown, and I knew he was my True One the moment I walked into his store. We moved in together eight months later and have not separated since.[1]

---

1 That's not to say I didn't continue having adventures of my own along the way, including one hell of a summer abroad.

Winged Skeletons

*I*n the summer of 1991 I lived with a murderer, an albino Elvis impersonator, and a girl whose TV told her she was wicked. I was in London as a volunteer working with mentally ill homeless people. All because in my junior year as a comparative literature major I worried that I'd chosen the wrong academic pursuit.

The desire to serve others was tugging at me. I even pondered changing my major to social work. Before doing that, though, I decided to spend the summer testing out a career in social services. I liked the thought of having a full-time vocation devoted to helping folks. Early on—whether throwing cigarettes to the convicts or driving the elderly black lady to the grocery store each week—Mama had emphasized the importance of doing good. And when you yourself have been what they call "needy," it makes you want to decrease the neediness in the world.

I learned about the London program from a flyer posted on campus. It sounded like a sweet deal to boot: The volunteer agency guaranteed a free flat and a generous food stipend (translation: beer money). Since this program was one of the Queen Mother's pet charities, the summer would culminate in a grand reception held at her estate. I really liked that part.

What could they possibly ask an untrained American college student to do? I imagined myself surrounded by charming English eccentrics who'd recently fallen on hard times. We'd sip cream tea and recite favorite Monty Python lines. Perhaps I'd stop at the pub after a strenuous afternoon of art therapy before strolling back to my swingin' London pad.

WRONG.

Smith Lodge was the euphemistic name for the nuthouse where I worked—and lived. It seemed that the flat fell through, so I was given an efficiency in the facility. As the only "staff" member there after four o'clock, I became the house mother to an unholy herd of schizophrenics, violent offenders, addicts, and HIV-positive prostitutes.

The murderer I mentioned had brutally beaten a man to death in a rainy alley forty years before. Mr. Thomas was now just a feeble old man who painted bad pictures of flowers and boats. He seemed benign until the day I ran into him on a double-decker bus.

He was straining to get my attention, but I couldn't tell what he wanted—his accent and ill-fitting dentures made his speech unintelligible. Becoming impatient and angry, he repeated himself once more before morphing into a monster. His eyes became filmy like green olives, and I felt an iron hand on my neck. Was this what the

man in the alley felt before Thomas split his head open?
I hotfooted it to the top of the bus.

Colin, the Elvis impersonator, didn't start off as an
Elvis impersonator. The twenty-one-year-old surfaced
at Smith Lodge right after I did. He was as thin as den-
tal floss and obsessed with destroying the building's
elevator.

Many nights I was jarred awake by screeches of "Lor-
reh-a, please stop him! He's banging on the lift again!"

I'd find Colin with his arms and face drenched in
black elevator grease. The streaks on his transparent white
face made him look like the warlord of the asylum.

Colin passed the time with Elvis songs, jittery ren-
ditions of "Hound Dog" and "Viva Las Vegas." Someone suggested that he perform for the patrons of the
pub across the street. He was a smash and became the
in-house entertainer. He didn't know the drunks were
actually making fun of him. It didn't matter though, because he became convinced that winged skeletons were
catbirding him. He had to be hospitalized. His breakdown affected me deeply. I started to realize that I was
too connected to his suffering to help him.

I did make some progress—finding grant money
to finance a resident's bike ride across England to raise
awareness for his disease: Tourette's syndrome. The disease can cause convulsions and vulgar outbursts. Andrew, always attired in glaring Spandex bike shorts, was
so thrilled about the grant that he cussed like a sailor and
collapsed in a shiny heap at my feet.

Despite the good news, I still fretted over his mental problems. In fact, I worried about everyone, and it was taking a toll. My doubts about becoming a social worker grew with each pint of Guinness I consumed—and eventually I consumed six pints every night. My main job was to be an advocate for the residents. The goal was to transition them from Smith Lodge to independent living. I learned my way around the most godforsaken areas of the city, inspecting urine-drenched council flats and locking horns with small-hearted bureaucrats. This was not Ben Jonson's London.

The other "success" story was Clyde, a four-foot-ten native of French Guiana and a gentle, sweet man. He had a severe stammer and was terrified of the outside world. It was determined that he was ready to live on his own, but he never would be—he needed a supportive community. He undermined everything I did to get his council flat ready.

We both cried when the moving van arrived to transport his belongings to his new home in London's equivalent of the Black Hole of Calcutta. I couldn't bear the cruelty of the situation. His few things—clothes, toiletries, a framed photo of his long-dead mother—looked lonely in the back of the spacious van.

Once he got settled in the flat, I walked to Kentucky Fried Chicken for a housewarming gift of Original Recipe. A punk tried to mug me on the way back. I was thrown to the ground, but Clyde's chicken was unruffled. I was so mad that I kicked the guy in the balls and started screaming bloody murder. I shot him birds with both hands as he fled.

I knew then and there that I'd never be a social worker. To paraphrase the labor activist Mother Jones, I was more hell-raiser than humanitarian. And I'd never have or want the emotional detachment—let alone the temperament—necessary for the job.

I'd crossed the Atlantic to see if I should spend my life in direct service to others. I left there seeing that this kind of work would destroy me—I was too empathetic. Too concerned about Colin, Andrew, and Clyde. In the end, I came to understand the old saying that if you live next to the cemetery, you can't cry for everyone.

Despite this, I was beside myself with excitement on my last day in London. I'd be home soon, and the much-anticipated reception at the Queen Mother's was to be held that evening. I cleaned my purple suede shoes and bought a silk hippie dress for the occasion. I was ironing the dress when the phone rang: It was someone calling to say the Queen Mum had canceled. Damn, just damn.

As I boarded the plane at Heathrow the next morning, I couldn't wait to get back to Athens and finish my literary studies. Now I knew I was on the right track but had no idea how I could possibly use it to do any good.

Wez-lee-an

*A*fter Jim and I graduated, he from grad school and me from undergrad, I was offered a public-relations job at Wesleyan College in Macon, Georgia. The position was a natural progression from the student job I had in research communications at UGA. Wesleyan is a highly respected private women's college. But in the early 1990s it was still a vestige of the old genteel South—the South that kept itself well-supped through the disenfranchisement of everyone else.

Special luncheons at Wesleyan were held in the formal parlors on campus. Usually a black man in white coat served tomato aspic and chicken salad. The women diners addressed him fondly and by his first name, like he was a loyal, beloved house Negro. I was mortified and uncomfortable on the one occasion I was in the parlor. I fit in there like Sambo at a Klan rally.

When I pronounced the name of the college "Wez-lee-an," I was corrected curtly by an elderly belle with puckered-butthole lips. "It is 'Wes (pause)-lee-an.' The name of our college does *not* rhyme with 'Lez-be-an.'"

On the one hand, I was glad to be starting a career, especially one not in a shirt or pants factory. But my six months at Wesleyan were an excruciating boondoggle. When another college PR job became available in Savannah, Jim and I had nothing to lose and were gone.

Gutters and Stars

We are all of us lying in the gutter, but some
of us are looking at the stars.

—OSCAR WILDE

There are plenty of nice neighborhoods in Savannah, but we couldn't afford to live in one. We were drowning in student-loan debt.

I lived in one of the town's tougher areas, in a part of Savannah that most never hear about—the rough river town with rats the size of breadbaskets. Where violent crime skulks just around the corner from the comely antebellum homes and tourist traps.

I was smack-dab in the middle of it, in an environment of people simmering and suffering—a habitat natural to me since childhood. The challenge was to figure out a better, more adult way to respond to it and learn from it.

It wasn't easy. On cold winter nights the downstairs neighbors busted up their furniture to use as kindling in the fireplace, a fireplace that hadn't been cleaned or inspected for twenty years. On another occasion these same neighbors fell asleep while sterilizing a pot of baby-bottle nipples on the stove. A fire erupted that made our place smell like a rubber factory in flames. Several weeks later, a black-booted fugitive squad met me at my door at four a.m. When they saw my pink-flamingo-print pajamas, the leader said through his ski mask, "Wrong person," and they left without further comment. This was routine business on East 40th Street.

And yet there were also people in the neighborhood who remained unfazed by the goings-on in Bedlam. They were loving, strong, and undisturbed—seemingly tuned in to another frequency, a phantom station. They operated on the higher end of the dial while the rest of us moved about in static.

Savannah was desperate and inspired. Flawed but enlightened. Wonderfully, deliciously decadent and gorgeous. She stirred something big inside my heart and mind. This unnameable something incubated over the seven years I lived there. The old city also nourished it, gave it shape. I had no clue about what was developing inside me, but it felt significant, like a sleeping giant. In fact, it was actually a slumbering queen. A Cracker Queen.

Way South of Normal

*M*avis Jenkins has chained the Baby Jesus up in her front yard again.

Twenty years ago somebody had snatched him from the Nativity display in her yard, and she was *not* gonna let that happen again. Somebody egged him too, but she said it wouldn't be right to swaddle the Savior in cling wrap.

Mrs. Jenkins, who, incidentally, was the longest-working Methodist church pianist in Georgia, was one of my neighbors in an area of Savannah with more stories per square foot than a confessional booth.

The Savannah I lived in was the one the Chamber of Commerce did *not* want you to know about. Empty crack bags littered the street. Crime was so bad that a group of old men formed a Geriatric Militia and patrolled the area at night with .45s and .38s on their laps. But the fact is I loved the theater that played out day and night—in the yards, streets, and porches. The neighborhood was sketchy, but its funk and diversity kept it lively and endearing.

The vibe started going dark, however, when new

people moved into the house behind mine. Months before they arrived, it had been a crack house and the site of a triple homicide. The killings were drug-related and savage. We wondered who in their right mind would want to rent a place with that history. The answer: equally notorious thugs involved in the same kinds of activities.

We called them the Dog Fighters because they kept half-starved pit bulls on short chains in their yard. Weights around their necks were intended to build muscle and viciousness. Only the meanest dogs win fights.

When it was time to take the dogs to a fight, they'd load them in the trunks of their Caprice Classics and slam the lid. This kept the animals out of sight and prevented them from dirtying the spotless interiors of their cars. They were careful to hide what they were doing. When I reported them, the police said they couldn't do anything if I hadn't seen a fight.

It wasn't long afterward that my life collided with the Dog Fighters. It started with the worst sound I have ever heard: the sound of a pit bull killing a puppy. I almost threw up.

It thrilled the crowd of onlookers in their backyard, however. Kids, parents, and old men pressed against the fence for a better view. A father hoisted his toddler in the air so that she could see too. They laughed, talked, and cheered on the pit bull, as if rooting for the heavyweight champion defending his title.

The Dog Fighters were trying to get their pit bull

hungry for the kill. I was relieved when their grand-mother emerged from the house. Surely she would stop it. But she just came out to say hey to somebody and bum a cigarette.

I yelled at them to break it up, but the ringleader wouldn't restrain the dog until I looked him in the eye with the craziest Cracker look that I could conjure. The puppy staggered a few feet and crumpled. In my head I heard my mother say, "There are a lot of things in this world worse than death."

For more than a year the Dog Fighters had terror-ized the neighborhood with their drug trade and vio-lence. We knew they were fighting dogs, but this was the first time I'd actually seen it. This signaled a new level of brutality.

Up until this point I'd made it my mission to show them that I was not afraid. That they would not destroy our community. Now I was beginning to doubt that.

Over the next few days I tried to learn more about what I'd witnessed in their backyard. I found some-one willing to talk about dog fighting. In fact, his eyes brightened as he gave me the scoop on all facets of the "sport"—the gambling, the kinds of dogs that make the best matches, the way exhausted dogs are shot up with drugs to keep them going, and, most of all, the exhilara-tion of watching it. "There's nothing more exciting than a good dog fight—a fight to the death."

After his testimonial I told him about the pit bull and the puppy. He gave me a funny look and asked where

The Cracker Queen 107

I lived—I realized that he knew the Dog Fighters well. That queasy feeling returned.

"You'd better be careful around them. They're very violent people," he said. "But they have a sorry pit bull. He's a sorry fightin' dog."

Our neighborhood mattered to us, but now I was wondering if we should just cut our losses and leave before we got hurt. Was it worth fighting for a place where people were entertained by a puppy losing its life?

Mama was right. There are lots of things worse than death. One of them is watching your home slowly being taken over by bad guys—and realizing that the crowd at the fence is cheering them on.

As the neighborhood continued to tank, most everyone who could got out. Left behind was a hodgepodge of purebred Southern kooks.

Like the man and his grown son who bicycled all day, wearing women's sun hats and blank turtle gazes, pedaling intently, going nowhere. And the Pole Artist. He used a telephone pole as his canvas, posting a bizarre jumble of biblical references and found objects. Late one night he carefully arranged slices of bread around the pole. I asked him about it but couldn't make sense of what he said. Great artists don't speak the same language as you and me.

Rounding off the block was a blind woman who reportedly ate live chickens—and the Gypsy King, a greasy guy who wore polyester suits and flashed rotten brown smiles underneath a jaunty driving cap. He was the head of a family of tinkers. I once saw him spray paint the rust on his car with paint from the Everything's a Dollar store.

The freaks were fun to watch. In fact, I counted myself among them. But not everyone was a nutcase, certainly not the queenpin who arose from this menagerie: Miss Martin.

She was a sight. Try to imagine a rutabaga wrapped in a floral house dress and that was Miss Martin.

Barely five feet tall, her knees quivered underneath 250 pounds of Southern-fried fat. She waddled, but she got around. At least she did when Mr. Higgins was in his prime. He was her dog—a homely, rotund pug with a constant tubercular cough.

Miss Martin walked Mr. Higgins five times a day on some of the most dangerous and seedy streets. It was a hard haul for her, but her whole life had been hard.

She covered a lot of ground on those walks—stopping to talk with the crack dealer next door, then crossing the alley to speak to the shady storefront preacher. She treated everyone with respect, moving through the day with a quiet joy. It was a ragged, mixed-up mess of a neighborhood, but she was a friend to all of us. When my water was cut off because the slumlord didn't pay the bill, she brought water to me—carrying a plastic jug in each hand, teetering like a seesaw.

I was invited to her sagging house many times. On the wall was a light-up Jesus whose bulbs had burned out years before. Miss Martin couldn't afford a clothes dryer, so she ran wires across the living room and hung her things there to dry. Once when I came over for supper, I had to duck underneath a massive line of underwear— or be knocked down by big-mama drawers the size and heft of circus tents.

Our suppers together always began the same way— we'd take our seats at the Formica table and wait for the macaroni and government cheese to finish baking. She'd heap sugar on her portion while it was fresh from the oven and still bubbling. Mr. Higgins took his with sugar as well.

One time for dessert she pulled a frozen pie out of a blank cardboard box. I recognized it instantly from the emergency food bank where I volunteered. A big black date stamped on the box warned that the pie had expired ten months earlier. I considered the possibility of food poisoning, but I wasn't about to hurt Miss Martin's feelings by refusing the pie.

She'd hurt enough in her life, raising four girls while living like a gypsy—moving their trailer from one campsite to another—always broke yet always working. Then when she did manage to get a home, it had to be in this place.

Years later when we left Savannah, we moved to a better neighborhood that wasn't nearly as good.

We were able to leave, but Miss Martin couldn't. There's nothing good about being poor or enduring the miseries that come from it. It breaks many more people than it strengthens. But not the Rutabaga Woman—Miss Martin might bend, but she never gave way.

At first I pitied the people who were stuck there—tethered like the pit bulls—by poverty, mental illness, and bad choices. But I soon realized that the bad guys might not win this one, because they were surrounded and outnumbered by folks who were either too crazy to be scared or too stubborn to budge.

The human spirit was prevailing there, but not in any made-for-TV, inspirational way. The meanest dogs would lose this fight—because Mavis Jenkins, the Geriatric Militia, and Miss Martin were all holding their ground.

It's Vacuous at the Top

*B*elieve it or not, the oddest part of living in Savannah wasn't the neighborhood. It was the alternate reality of my professional life. By day I'd direct a communications/PR office on a liberal arts campus and then drive home to an entirely different world.

Thanks to a marvelous president named Bob Burnett, I moved up quickly at the university. Being young and female, I encountered resistance from senior administrators who resented that I'd been given a place at their table. One vice president didn't make eye contact with me for six months. Still, I worked hard to prove myself and continued my ascension.

Mama was proud to have a career girl. While on my way to an out-of-town business meeting, I stopped at her place for lunch. As soon as she spied me in my business suit and heels, she grabbed the camera and took a dozen photos—before I had even made it inside her trailer. When I walked back outside to use my cell phone, she rushed me like paparazzi. She had to capture the image of her "executive" daughter on this newfangled phone.

By this time Mama and her boyfriend Tom were living together, and life had become much easier. Tom was financially secure, so Mama didn't have to struggle anymore. Our relationship was a loving one, but she was still drinking. As long as alcohol was involved, we'd never be whole.

The university job gave me financial stability as well. It was awfully comforting to be able to pay bills on time and have some extra money at the end of the month. I also delighted in the creative freedom I was allowed. Public relations is just another form of storytelling, so I suppose it makes sense that I ended up in that field. By the age of twenty-eight, I'd reached the so-called top.

In getting there I got a crash course in human nature—the side that's obsessed with position, title, and empire-building. The administrators engaged in constant turf wars, always jockeying for power and attacking each other in attempts to seize more control. They were duplicitous—smiling in your face as they plotted your downfall. It was a viper's den, but it made me tougher and stronger. The groveling and sucking up were so loud you could hear shoes shuffling and lips locking on fat, white asses.

The overriding question I had once I got to the "pinnacle" was, "Oh come on—is this all there is? Is this what they want to hold on to at all costs? And how could folks their age still be playing these joy-robbing games?"

For some their title was their entire identity. I knew that I wanted to do more and have a fuller life. When on my deathbed, I certainly wouldn't be thinking about how I streamlined a process or wrote an award-winning annual report.

The thought of staying in that job, or any job, for thirty years made the blood drain from my head. And as I moved higher, I became more and more separated from the creative work—the fun stuff. I need to create like I need to breathe. But instead I was attending soul-sapping committee meetings and getting increasingly antsy.

As a teenager I had some low-level jobs, but at least they all had life to them. This university job was starting to feel colder than Lenin's cadaver, especially once President Burnett retired.

Before college I'd worked as a horse photographer's assistant, a tarot card reader, and a typist for the Warner Robins newspaper. The summer after my freshman year at UGA, I was a cocktail waitress in a bar called the Fizz Lounge. (Truth is, it had gone flat a good decade earlier.) I didn't want to go back to any of those jobs, but in some ways they were better than where I found myself.

Racing up the career track turned out to be a blessing. It showed me that reaching the top wasn't the end-all, be-all. In fact, it made me hunger for a richer life and freed me from further professional ambitions. It helped that Savannah was eccentric and surprising and mysterious. My day job might have turned boring and bland, but its effects were tempered by Savannah's charms and quirks.

In Savannah there's no shortage of playful mischief under the surface of things. Mischief that defies reason, logic, or normal explanation. This might account for why the city has a reputation for being haunted. Other worlds are at work there.

Should you visit Savannah, don't trust what you see in mirrors or shop windows. It's a place where true reflections are few and far between.

You Put a Root on Me

African folk magic has been alive and well in Savannah since the first slaves brought it there in the eighteenth century. If you know what to look for, you can see it everywhere—on the porches, door frames, and windowsills painted Haint Blue, an unmistakable blue-green believed to block evil spirits—or haints—from entering. In wavy lines drawn on a dirt path. And in a downtown business that sells minerals and powders for use in spells and jinxes. Yes, there's that much of a market for hoodoo in Savannah.

Occasionally, signs of hoodoo would emerge from details in the crime reports. I remember the account of a dead gentleman found nude in a bathtub, his mouth crammed with chicken parts. His body emptied of all blood. It was determined that he'd died a natural death. Never an explanation of who took the blood or how, just that the blood was drained and the mouth stuffed after he died. Hmmm . . .

Twice during my time in Savannah a severed human hand or foot was discovered. But when the rightful owner of said extremity was tracked down, he'd tell some cockamamie story.

"No, Officer, I don't know how that foot of mine came off. Sure don't . . . I can't recall."

What else could the police do? Case closed.

Professional hoodoo practitioners are sometimes referred to as root doctors or root workers because they use herbs for magical purposes. I'd heard of such people, of course, but never suspected one would ever "throw a root" on me. But that is what happened.

It was a Wednesday when the root was put on me. It worked fast, too. By that night "it" had begun: a strange series of accidents and near-death calamities.

We had been living in Savannah for six years, and I was still working at the university. In looking for that richer life I desired, I had become a part-time columnist for the town's alternative newspaper. The editor let me cover whatever I wanted, and I delighted in ridiculing and railing against politicians and city policies. On that particular Wednesday my article criticizing a local senator hit the stands. Apparently in Savannah, this kind of thing not only gets you blackballed, it gets a black candle burned in your name.

That evening I took a run with my dog, a husky mix named Elsie. In a flash I tripped and slammed into the pavement. This triggered an innate Iditarod urge in Elsie and she bolted, dragging me a good ten feet.

I was still facedown on the blacktop when I felt the heat of headlights on my back; a runaway taxi almost flattened us.

I hobbled home bloody and burned and with a hole

in my knee. Limping with red-streaked arms and legs, I wondered if I looked like a short stand-in for Jack Nicholson in *The Shining*. Minutes later I heard a deep growl coming from a bush: There stood a teeth-baring black dog, the ultimate symbol of bad mojo.

But I had no idea about the root at that time. I thought it was just bad Irish Cracker luck, like the time a year earlier when I was whacked in the face by a falling railroad tie.

Anyhow, the doctor who treated the burns assured me that I could go on a planned trip to the West Coast the next day. But "it" continued.

Upon descent into Salt Lake City, our jet hit a vertical air mass. Passengers prayed out loud in the languages of their birth. Emergency lights blazed the plane's interior. All the while I was sitting next to a yoga instructor who was at complete peace about her imminent death. This didn't help me one bit. Here I was from Jesus Land sitting next to the Buddha. I wanted to cry and sing, *"Will the circle be unbroken—by and by Lord, by and by,"* but in the end all she could offer me was a slice of her organic sunflower bread.

After changing planes in Salt Lake City, I continued on to Portland, Oregon, to attend a conference. The stress of travel made my physical condition worsen. My ankles had swollen like pickled pig's feet in a jar. My body throbbed more than a neon sign at a pay-by-the-hour motel.

Too sick to participate in the conference, I stayed in

bed and tried to build up my strength for the last leg of the trip: a visit to Seattle to see a friend.

An extraordinary woman sat next to me on the train to Seattle. In the beginning, nothing seemed special or unusual about her other than that she was visibly pregnant. We made small talk until she noticed my bandaged knee and asked what happened. I described my freak accident and the resulting burns on my arms and shins. Then I explained how my knee was damaged by a rock in the road. I wallowed in the details.

She said she knew what rocks and burns felt like and told me what happened on the first day of her honeymoon. She and her new husband were speed biking down a steep hill when her bike hit a rock in the road, causing an awful tumbling crash—leaving her with broken bones and second- and third-degree burns over her entire body. She was as pink and helpless as a newborn for months.

As she spoke, I became so ashamed of myself for whining about my problems—which I could now see weren't even tall enough to stand in the shadow of hers. Hearing the details of her hardship made mine light—like atoms floating away in ether.

She then went on to reveal that she was dying of placental cancer. That her unborn son would have to be taken if she were to have a slim chance of survival. A lump the size of a cannonball grew in my throat. She talked at length about how she'd beaten cancer years before—and how she'd yearned to be a mother. I hoped that it gave her some measure of comfort, some release, to tell her story to a stranger, somebody she'd never have to deal with or see again. I was grateful to hear every word, to be in her presence, which increasingly took on the quality of a spirit or divine visitor. I knew that I was receiving something profound.

The views from the train window were beautiful: verdant forests, sparkling lakes. But then an ominous image appeared: a huge nuclear power plant right in the middle of the landscape. It reminded me of the nature of things—how you can be coasting along just fine until life throws a rock on your road. It always finds a way to find you, no matter the path you take.

Things improved when I got to my friend's house in Seattle, but I confided to him that I didn't feel right—like someone had a black candle over my head. That's exactly what I said, despite knowing nothing about the root.

Before long I was able to bend my knee again, and the burns were healing. We celebrated over breakfast at a sunny café and toasted to my turnaround with a lovely salmon frittata. But by the second bite, however, I smelled burning sulfur and tasted blood: One of my front teeth had fallen out. What's more, the emergency dentist I went to said he couldn't fix it and that I'd need to see my own dentist back home. So there I stood: a bad Southern stereotype in Seattle—a toothless woman from Georgia named Lo-retta.

My only solace was the words of Winston Churchill: "If you're going through hell, keep going."

Well, that and the woman on the train. I remembered her bravery, her total lack of self-pity, the unimaginable suffering. I recalled everything she said and how she said it.

I pictured her standing there like a superhero with her baby son on her back. They're smiling and wearing matching blue capes. She aims some sort of cosmic ray gun at me—its chamber loaded with the words she spoke that day. She squeezes the trigger and BAM—my troubles are zapped down to size. This fantasy made me take my problems in stride.

Back home in Savannah I learned that a supporter of the senator I had criticized said he'd worked a root on me and that bad things would happen. I acted cool about it to my friends and said it was just a coincidence. But at nightfall I crossed the creaky bridges over to coastal South Carolina, hoodoo's ground zero—the place where it is most alive—and met up with a root doctor of my own.

I didn't know if roots had any power, but I was covering all the bases. Candles were lit, and protection was conjured. No more can be said, as I had to agree not to reveal what I witnessed. But I will say this: There wasn't a whole lot to it. It's way better in the movies.

My root doctor wore creased jeans, a polo shirt, and glasses. He was so nondescript that I could picture him going to a day job as a government accountant. Or serving as a deacon at his church. In this part of the country, people shift seamlessly between realms.

When I got back to my house later that night, I prayed to my God for protection before going to bed. And the next morning I felt like my old self again. The spate of bad luck was over. Something must have worked—whether it was root doctoring or prayer or something else.

Maybe it was the woman on the train. Listening to her was like a baptism: It took me under, cleansed me, and opened a door to grace.

Pinkie's Is Closed on Sundays!

In the shadow of Savannah's cathedral is a dingy bar called Pinkie Master's. Some people worship at the cathedral. My people worship at Pinkie's.

The décor includes a 1949 photo of George Wallace in his amateur boxing days. To the left, a spotlight shines directly on a painting of a nude woman's backside. The late-night crowd ranges from scars on barstools to the cotillion girls. Art-school students and young professionals go there to be cool. But the cadre that gathers between four and six p.m. are the truest cool ones: Bill, Gene and Pat, Gordon, and several others.

Bill is my dear comrade. He is at least twenty years my senior, wears black horn-rimmed glasses, and has hair like Einstein's. At first we met at Pinkie's to deride and lampoon the administration of the university where we both worked. Soon our conversations expanded to literature, classical music, and other things of great import, such as the company of dogs, growing a perfect key lime, and the ways in which black folks were advanced over whitey.

That was the freedom of Pinkie's—you could say

anything and be anything there. Queer men held hands under the nudie painting; George Wallace didn't utter a peep to the interracial couples in his booth. Sexists, racists, and phobes of all sorts inhabited the bar, and they were allowed their due, too. It was the kind of place where you could admit to killing a man and no one would tell. Confess to harming an animal, though, and expect trouble. Pinkie's had standards.

Crossing over the threshold of the establishment, I always felt my blood pressure drop and shoulders loosen. Its effects were akin to a massage, and that's before you order the first drink. The bar was a legendary haven for Savannahians who were wound a bit too tight—an ideal setting for airing one's frustrations and questions. As long as you expressed yourself honestly, you'd find a respectful audience. Bullshitters, on the other hand, were shut down faster than a whorehouse in Utah. This kept the quality of discourse unusually high.

Bill had once been the speechwriter for the head of a federal agency; he even had his own room at the Library of Congress. While working at the university, he brought internationally renowned literary scholars to campus. That was in his heyday, but by the time I met him, his heyday was as dusty as the archaic curtains at Pinkie's. They'd disintegrate if ever touched.

It wasn't long before the university administration turned his job to dust, and he had to make ends meet by becoming a substitute teacher in South Carolina, in a school system raging with dysfunction and black-on-white racism. Now without insurance, he got his health care from a free clinic for the poor. But he focused on the beauty around him: the output of his tomato plants; his dogs, Winston and Basil; local oysters and coastal sunsets. And, of course, music.

"It doesn't get any better than that, kiddo!" he'd say.

Bill's values were mine, too. Before raising our plastic cups at Pinkie's, I'd go to the jukebox and play "Me and Bobby McGee" by Janis Joplin. This was the ceremonial beginning to every visit. I'd listen in reverent silence to the whole song.

Don't be misled: Bill and I could yammer with the best of 'em. Sometimes we'd be there for hours and hours, consuming baskets of house popcorn, which Pinkie's made spicy by adding Tabasco to the cooking oil. Cheap beer never found a tastier companion.

We'd tell funny and distressing stories about our past while trying to decipher the present. When the pressure of my neighborhood started to clamp down on me, I could go there and get perspective on the meanness and the pain. Pinkie's helped me to unclutter my brain so I could pierce through to the important parts. Talking it all out, I became convinced that I wanted to live like Miss Martin and the other exceptional folks, the ones tuned into a higher frequency.

I made notes on cocktail napkins and cobbled together an initial set of core values: fearlessness, authenticity, service, and a rip-roaring sense of humor. I had already learned these values while growing up, but Savannah demanded that I shine them up and shift them into overdrive.

As I hashed out this model for how I wanted to live, four additional values outranked all the others: love, forgiveness, thankfulness, and purpose. I realized that everything good flowed from those, and when they were missing, so was your joy. Writing these ideas down and sharing them with the people at Pinkie's enabled me to see what I wanted to become and what I didn't. My model for life would call for fierce manifestations of these principles, not diluted kumbaya crap. Years of epiphanies at that bar forged my identity as a Cracker Queen.

The owner of Pinkie's was a Queen herself. In her prime, Miss Ruby had been Savannah's Marilyn Monroe. Platinum hair, heavy lids, showy dresses in solid orange, purple, teal, yellow, red, with matching heels and jewelry. Her dresses had plunged and cinched. She had been an attraction and she knew it; she played it out. Old men quaked at the memory of how she va-voomed through Forsyth Park, rolling her shoulders, twisting her peach of a rear. Not only a wonder to behold, she was equally smart and witty. You'd do anything for her, but she didn't abuse her radiant power.

By the time I met her, she was a lumpy old lady who wore bedroom slippers to the bar. But her stylish Marilyn hair and pretty features remained. When she entered the bar, it was as if the house lights were suddenly doused and the spotlight moved from the nude painting directly to her. She was most certainly still an attraction, albeit a fleeting one because she never stayed long enough. We were always left craving more of her centrifugal charm.

I'm sure she was the one responsible for doing the particularly nice things done for the regulars. There was the annual Christmas potluck party during which patrons drank anything they wanted, on the house. The dispensing of free mint juleps during the Kentucky Derby. You could also work out a payment plan if your long-overdue tab started to resemble a historic document. Have a long drive home? No worries, Pinkie's would hide your to-go beverage in a brown bag.

One night I consumed a few extra Pabst Blue Ribbons and headed to the powder room. While en route I spied a man winking at me. He was short, spry, and had a mischievous glint in his eye. On my way back to the bar, he was there again, in the same spot, winking for the second time. What the hell, I returned a playful wink and rejoined Bill.

Once I sobered up I realized that the guy was pretty two-dimensional—made of cardboard, in fact. I'd been flirting with a cardboard cut-out leprechaun, a life-size advertisement for Irish whiskey.

Like Savannah itself, Pinkie's served up a profane spirituality. Jesus hung out with prostitutes and made wine, Bill said. Although Miss Ruby's body now drooped and dragged, she glowed as she ministered to a congregation of cynical believers, people who'd never set foot inside a regular church.

Her establishment certainly spurred on my spiritual growth. Toward the end of my run in Savannah, I'd surfaced as a fully formed, and some might say formidable, Cracker Princess. I wasn't quite a Queen yet, but I knew what my brand of Queendom looked like. It resembled the bar: It was loud and not always pretty. More pockmarked than perfect, but its heart was pure.

During open-mic night at a coffee shop, a guy read a poem he titled "Pinkie's Is Closed on Sundays!" I laughed because I knew exactly what he meant. We needed, and I mean needed, it to be open every day of the week. That dirty, skanky joint replenished us.

I imagine that the cathedral across the square offered the traditional Catholic "bells and smells." At Pinkie's, however, it was all clinks and stinks. But like the Janis Joplin song says, the one that opened each of *our* services, Buddy, that was good enough for me.

Miss Vassie Thompson Has a Spare Room for an Elderly Person

I was at Pinkie's when the Weather Channel reported that a Category 5 hurricane would make a direct hit on Savannah. I didn't have to hear it twice. I got the hell out of Dodge.

I'm not one of those stubborn holdouts in times such as those. You know, the ones who stay behind and greet you smugly when it's over. No, when you think twelve-foot waves are about to decimate your house and its contents, you're forced to quickly decide what's most worth saving, and whatever it is has to fit in the car. In my case, it was my two cats, the dog, the ashes of another cat, a family Bible, and a few photos. Off we raced to Mama's welcoming doublewide in Dublin, Georgia. Jim had to join us later, as his job at a state prison required that he stay with the inmates.

I'd always liked Dublin, but it revealed an uncommon graciousness when five thousand Savannahians, fleeing from the hurricane, showed up on its doorstep. The town opened its homes, campers, churches, tanning salons, schools, and barns to the evacuees.

When asked why, a resident looked incredulous, as

if the answer was plainly obvious. "This is a small town; we take care of people."

I couldn't believe how the town mobilized so quickly and completely.

A radio station broadcast the names and numbers of local Samaritans offering accommodations: "Miss Ola Tanner has two bedrooms, hot baths, and food. . . . Mr. Charlie Mobley has horse stables and an Airstream trailer available. . . . Vassie Thompson of Highway 29 has a spare room for an elderly person. . . . This just in: the Pentecostal Campground has been opened for evacuees. Call Brother Ray for directions."

The outpouring was so large that DJs had to break in every fifteen minutes. While weary travelers awaited the next update, they played country and gospel classics like Hank Williams's "I Saw the Light." It seemed the entire town cared.

The Lions Club grilled hamburgers on Main Street until everyone was fed. Veterinarians boarded animals for free. Food was delivered to refugees who had pulled into parking lots to rest their sagging SUVs.

Savannah city buses rolled along rural roads named after men who had probably never set foot inside Savannah. The buses were packed with destitute families, the homeless, the mentally ill. Churches flung wide their doors to these people and gave what was for some of them the finest reception of their lives. The least truly did go first.

I'd never seen anything like it—a community that

was embodying the arch-values I'd assembled at Pinkie's. And in classic Cracker Queen fashion, they were transmuting a potentially horrendous situation into one of goodwill and love.

Mama and I visited Bethlehem Baptist Church, where elaborate preparations were under way as the church was being converted to a shelter. Homemade chicken and dumplins simmered on the stove. Dumplins rolled out by hand by a large country woman named Ethel or Lurleen or Big Mama. A constant stream of church members arrived with hot dishes and Jell-O molds. There would be a feast fit for a king. The drama team and youth choir provided after-dinner entertainment. It was like Mayberry but better: This was real.

Before nightfall a makeshift shower had been constructed outside the shelter. Pieces of plywood formed the shower's ramshackle walls, and a garden hose was rigged over the top. Somebody dubbed it the Redneck Shower.

A number of folks at the church shelter barely made it, due to raggedy cars and no cash. A lady said she hadn't eaten that well in years and didn't want to go back home. One man had such a high-lonesome despairing look that Mama and I pooled our funds and gave them to him. We understood that look.

I was lucky to have Mama to go to when the evacuation was ordered. She had moved from Warner Robins to Dublin in order to be closer to her grandson Dusty, my sister Donna's son. She stopped drinking, and everything changed for the better. Mama's place was finally what it should be: a warm, safe, stable environment.

Donna had given her an ultimatum: Either stay sober or don't see your grandson again. Mama claims to have "just lost the taste" for beer, but her sudden disinterest coincided with Donna's warning. Further, Mama became a spectacular grandmother. Her love for Dusty overpowered her lust for alcohol.

She was such a fixture at all of Dusty's softball games through the years that she is still known around town as Team Grandma. She even found peace with her own mother. No more questions about why she wasn't loved.

Similarly, the love that Dublin showed the evacuees brought us together—for a minute or two. This is historic because Savannah is famously tribal and clannish. Think Hutu and Tutsi but wielding martinis rather than machetes. And I'm just referring to high society. If you're not a direct descendant of General James Oglethorpe's party of founding fathers, then you can never wear the mantle of "Old Savannah."

In Dublin, though, the caste system evaporated for a luminescent moment. For once we were all brothers in the same situation, forced from our homes and facing an unfathomable threat. For once the thugs weren't trying to carjack the middle-class folks. The middle-classers weren't avoiding eye contact with the bums. And Old Savannah was making new friends with people they wouldn't deign to talk to again when things returned to normal. But that was progress for Old Savannah.

Thankfully the hurricane bypassed Savannah. As soon as the all-clear was given, Dublin's visitors loaded up their dogs and in-laws and headed back to the coast. I told Mama bye and prepared to drive away. At the last minute, she leaned her head inside the car and said, "I love you the most."

"No, I love you the most."

When I got a few hundred feet away, I honked the horn at least twenty times. Short, staccato honks alternating with longer ones—like Morse code or a line of music. This was my way of singing. A song of joy: giddiness over having a home in Savannah to return to and in the rearview mirror a mother redeemed.

Cordell

Not long after the hurricane scare, life in Savannah returned to abnormal. Then I made a new friend in the neighborhood. His name was Cordell.

I met him when he hurled rocks through my stained-glass window. Thinking someone was shooting into the room, I ran outside and there he was: a skinny, four-foot-tall gangsta wannabe. His baggy pants hung so low that his belt was clearly embarrassed. He wore the color of the Eastside Gang, a menacing presence in that part of Savannah. Once confronted, he swore he didn't break the window and turned away, revealing a back pocket bulging with more rocks. I know it takes a village, but as far as I was concerned, his little black ass was grass.

Speaking of grass, a few months later he came by to ask if he could mow the lawn. He gave me a quote of thirty dollars to cut an area smaller than a midget's blanket. I decided to give him a chance, and we haggled until I held firm at twenty.

His lawnmower was hungry. It chewed up an extension cord and shredded the dog toys in the yard. He hid the evidence and then acted like he was owed thirty bucks. What a player.

The ten-year-old mini-thug also asked when he could return. Inexplicably, I told him to check back in two weeks. This is how our relationship continued: He made my yard look like hell and I paid him dearly for it.

During this time Cordell spray painted gang symbols on the street, stole my bike, and damaged my car. All of it stopped when I threatened to end our business dealings. He wasn't about to sever the tie that financed his preteen luxuries.

Two years passed. We talked sometimes after he mowed my grass. We worked together in the yard. We became friends. Yet he still tried to scam me. There we'd be, sitting on the porch, on the verge of a Hallmark moment, and he'd attempt to sell me a used lottery game card. Or he'd ask for a cash advance. "Miss Lo-retta, I can have five dollars?"

Unbeknownst to him, I was preparing to leave Savannah. Jim and I felt it was just time to go. We'd be moving to the suburbs of Atlanta, and I'd be working at a college in the city. After seven years in this neighborhood, I was tired of being an urban warrior and looking forward to the placid life in the burbs.

When I told Cordell I was leaving, he asked how many days were left. He rolled his eyes upward while counting on his fingers: Obviously he was doing a little financial planning.

He showed up on moving day and was underfoot

the whole time. His brothers Maurice and Vaughn were there too. I had not asked for help, so I wondered why they were there, pitching in so earnestly. Then I figured it out—of course—the little operator realized this was his last chance to score some big cash. I'll show him, I thought. This is the one time he is not getting *anything* out of me.

It was late when we finally loaded the van. I was hours behind, and the house had to be mopped. There he was, pestering me again. "Miss Lo-retta, I can mop the house? I can mop the whole house for ya."

My last nerve was shot. "Cordell—I am *not* giving you *any* money!"

His quiet reply stopped me dead. "I know, Miss Lo-retta."

It took everything I had not to burst into tears. I wanted to run to him, hug him, tell him I loved him, I'd miss him. Tell him to please not become a statistic. To stay in school. To stay out of the gang.

But I didn't. I saw that he already knew those things, the very things we had never spoken of.

Bad Day at Work

I t's hard to see when a crackhead is on your hood. Even more so when she's bleeding all over the windshield. This might sound like a scene from Savannah, but it happened in Atlanta, where I now worked.

This incident was the culmination of a really bad day. It began when I tripped and fell on my face in the office. Shaken by the accident, I decided to take an early lunch at my favorite restaurant, a home-cooking place that smells just like Me-Maw's kitchen.

While en route to the restaurant, a homeless dog darted in front of my car, but I managed to miss him. The car behind me did not. A large population of stray dogs roams the area, and nothing upsets me more than seeing them suffer. . . . Nothing except seeing one struck by a driver yakking on a cell phone. I wondered if I could stomach any food.

The restaurant has a unique character that reflects the community it serves. One of the waiters operates an illegal lottery on the premises. The duffel bag at his station contains fat rolls of cash. Clients sit in his section so they can "play the number," also known as "runnin' the bug." Atlanta's underground lottery has been known forever as the Bug.

That day the waitresses were laughing about a carjacker getting shot in the butt in the parking lot. The hapless thug didn't know that cops and detectives eat at the restaurant daily. When he bailed from the stolen car, he became an easy target because his low-riding pants kept him from running fast. The bullet didn't cause serious injury, but his gangsta bravado was mortally wounded. A bunch of gawkers had gathered, and when the paramedic removed his underwear, exposing his behind, they roared. Then came an onslaught of rear-end-themed taunts.

"Your black ass didn't have any business carjacking those people in the first place!"

"That'll teach your ass!"

"Maybe next time your black ass will think twice before you perpetrate."

The story was so funny and just what I needed. I was feeling better as I headed back to work. The feeling evaporated, though, as a strange sight came into view: two junkies pummeling a crackhead on the sidewalk.

Two-on-one isn't fair, and the crackhead was getting a thrashing. I slowed down to where they were and yelled, "I'm calling the police!"

They then knocked the woman so hard that she landed on my hood with her face smushed against the windshield. Blood gushed from her nose and mouth.

"I am calling the police now!" I reiterated.

They heard me this time, and their response shocked me. All three stopped everything and said, "No man, no need to call the cops. We a'ight." The attackers even helped the crackhead off the hood. Huh? Well who was I to disturb the law of the streets? Before I could leave, I had to use wiper fluid to wash away blood and clumps of hair weave.

A year of so after this event, and at almost the same spot in the road, I passed a situation that was about to turn tragic. Again I was returning to work after lunch when I saw that the cops had pulled a car over. I looked in the car as I went by and saw two people familiar to me: They were students at the college where I worked. I'd never see one of them again.

After I drove by, the student in the driver's seat was shot and killed by the officers who thought he was reaching for a gun. He had carjacked the vehicle at gunpoint but was unarmed when they stopped him. The photo on his student ID showed an enraged man dressed in a camouflage jacket. He looked lost, like he never even knew he was a child of God. He was named for the prophet Zephaniah, whose message was one of coming woes, of the impending judgment of the Lord.

The next day was a sad one when we got word of his death. Someone who knew him said it was probably a case of suicide by cop. No one claimed the body. No one questioned the police. The community and media barely took notice.

My campus has weathered other tough days as well.

A massive SWAT team descended on us once, with guns drawn, in search of a student who was an alleged international cocaine trafficker. The student had been tipped off and was long gone. The SWAT guys left like a hurricane out of breath.

You've probably surmised by now that my college is no ordinary one. Mine is a state technical college located in one of the poorest parts of Atlanta. Teenage prostitutes sashay up and down our street, and it's dicey to get gas at certain convenience stores. But our doors are open to everyone. Although the first choice of plenty, we are the last and only chance for many.

The students come to us with desperate problems: homelessness, physical and mental disabilities, felony convictions, addictions. We have refugees who survived ax attacks, village burnings, and torture and are now grappling with post-traumatic stress disorder.[1] Ours is a daunting job: to help make them strong at the broken places. We don't always succeed.

Untreated mental illness is a common culprit. From a student who "smelled the voodoo they were cooking up against her" in the financial aid office to the Jamaican immigrant who signed his name "Point Blank" before becoming psychotic and removing his clothes, the campus can be on edge at any time.

---

1 I should note that this does not describe our typical student. The average enrollee is not beset by any of these problems. They complete their studies and do just fine in the world. I choose not to write about them because I don't find their stories as compelling. As Queen Tammy Wynette put it, "The sad part about happy endings is that there's nothing to write about."

I've never seen a place where tears and prayers flow in such quantity or where Jesus is more loved. His name is invoked all day, every day. When things work out well, someone might say, "Honey, Jesus showed up and showed out, didn't he now!"

The Jesus talk was a turnoff for a while, but after years in that atmosphere, I now gladly take my dose of Jesus at the water fountain, in the break room, over the copy machine, wherever. Flannery O'Connor wrote about the Christ-Haunted South, but this takes it to a new level. I have to admit that it's gotten through to me and made me better. Belief in him is probably what holds the campus together some days.

That and an earnest desire on the part of the students to improve their lives. Ola Morgan, a seventh-grade dropout, personifies this notion. Although in her seventies and employed full-time, she attends night classes. When asked why, she looks at you like you've asked the dumbest question in the world and answers, "I don't want to die ignorant."

The college occasionally attracts famous and nearly infamous students such as an Olympic gold medalist and relatives of H. Rap Brown, the former Justice Minister of the Black Panthers and convicted cop killer.

This may sound strange, but the most exceptional students are the ones you find asleep in the hallways early in the morning. They are overnight shift workers who come straight to school from work and snooze for a few minutes before their eight a.m. class.

Our students are hungry for as many skills as they can get. It's common for them to leave us with credentials in various fields. An alumnus drives a van that advertises his multitudinous services. It reads:

PRESSURE WASH

WE BUY HOUSES

ELECTRICAL

BARBER

There's something to be said for that kind of diversification. Coming from a university background, I had never witnessed such entrepreneurship.

Our students take tremendous pride in their accomplishments, and so they should. I'll never forget watching the woman walking uphill in high heels on her way to campus. She was alone and dressed to the nines. If it had been me, I would have had to ditch the heels just to be able to trudge up the treacherous hill. But she carried herself like she was on the way to her own coronation.

An honors student, she was going to be recognized for academic excellence at a ceremony that morning. She was hours early because she had to catch the subway and two buses. When you're celebrating your transformed self, old barriers don't seem so steep. She was now overcoming them in six-inch stilettos.

Last year two psychics were on campus to give free mini-readings as part of a student event. They saw more than two hundred students. As I walked the psychics to their cars afterward, they remarked that in their combined forty years of reading fortunes, they'd never seen a group of people in such intense and profound spiritual development. I smiled. They affirmed what I already knew.

The truth is that the bad days at work are the best, too, because they remind me of the urgency of our mission. It goes far deeper than education: We are soul warriors.

During the graduation ceremony there is a constant buzz and hum in the air that isn't coming from the PA system. It is the sound of the Universe expressing its supreme contentment.

Thank you, Jesus. You showed up and you showed out again.

Scooterpootin'

*V*isits home have proven to be the antidote for the ills of Atlanta. More than anything, time there reminds me of who I am. Being close to the people and places of childhood has also revealed something surprising: I have not evolved into a Cracker Queen—I've been one from the beginning. Each trip home just verifies it.

When I go home, we always hit the thrift stores, flea markets, used-item emporiums, and ride around town—Mama calls it scooterpootin'. We never go to regular retail establishments, because Mama considers anyone who buys new things at full price to be a sucker.

Donna, my aunt Lanelle, or Dusty usually joins us on our leisurely rides. One time Donna had just returned from the eye doctor and couldn't see a thing. But when she insisted on driving us around town, we let her. She's still a bad-ass, and she is obeyed. She could have gotten a citation for DWB—driving while blind—but we'd rather risk our lives than tick her off. While shopping at the Goodwill Thrift Store that day, she walked by and greeted me like an acquaintance.

"Donna, it's me—your sister Retta," I said.

"Oh, you know I can't see too good today—I thought you were this stuck-up girl I know from River Wall."

The best part of scooterpootin' is the running commentary between Mama and them. Certain to be talked about are people who have suffered gory deaths; sightings of town characters; animal run-ins; and highlights from the crime report printed in the paper.

Deaths You Wouldn't Wish on Your Worst Enemy

The Gory Death Tales begin with a huge black stain on the bridge we're about to cross. Mama brings it to our attention.

"A grandmother and her little grandchildren were burned alive right there on that spot. The car just went up in blazes and that was all she wrote. Burned beyond recognition. The ashes are all that's left."

Silence. Then we strain to get a better view of the stain.

People in the country meet their Maker in ways that never touch the suburbs: They get squished, boiled, ensnared, or torn apart with alarming frequency. While we meander through a downtown neighborhood, Donna points out the home of a guy who fell into a chemical vat at one of the industrial plants in a nearby county.

"They couldn't fish him out right away because of the acids in the chemicals eatin' him up, you know."

That reminds us of when Donna worked at a factory and found a homeless man crushed to death. He had been asleep in an empty railroad car near Atlanta when several tons of cargo were dumped on top of him. Donna's job was to unload cargo, but she unloaded more than she'd bargained for. The poor man's body wasn't noticed until it was on a conveyor belt headed toward a vat. In his pocket was a citation for vagrancy. Donna and I talked on the phone that night, and she couldn't figure out why she had such a bad headache. That same day in Savannah a human hand was found in the park near my house.

Bartender, I'd Like a Hairy Lady with a Munchkin Chaser

On each visit home I ask about one person in particular— a man who dresses in drag and races his bike around town with a German shepherd galloping beside him. Aunt Lanelle reports that she saw him at the mental-health clinic and that he has taken to wearing a shorter wig that is quite becoming.

Dusty was four years old when he first saw this guy. While he was playing under a rack at the Salvation Army Thrift Store, this "woman" came up to peruse the dresses there. That was when Dusty got a faceful of "her" legs, and they were as hairy as a lumberjack's. As his eyes got bigger, the legs got closer. The long prickly hairs were about to gouge his eyes out when he hightailed it to his mother's side.

The most sensational adventure we had while scooterpootin' was when we went hunting for a munchkin. Not any munchkin: the Lead Munchkin in a scene from *The Wizard of Oz.*

Mama read in the paper that the munchkin had retired to Dublin, but she couldn't remember his name. She did recall that he lived in a nursing home or senior facility, and she was fairly certain about which one.

When we arrived there we realized that we should act like we knew him. Otherwise, they wouldn't allow a bunch of munchkin groupies in his room. I approached an employee in the hallway.

"Hi, could you direct me to Mr. . . . . oh, his last name always escapes me . . . you know, the munchkin from *The Wizard of Oz*?"

Without hesitation she told us he was in room 103. We were pumped up about seeing Dublin's most famous celebrity. Mama swooped down on the man, hugging him and telling him how much she loved him in the movie. He was old and in a wheelchair, so naturally she yelled at him. She has always yelled at the blind, the elderly, the mentally disabled, the wheelchair-bound, and foreigners.

"Do I know you?" asked the frail man.

"No, but I sure know you," she bellowed. "Your movie has given me so much enjoyment through the years. It's an honor to meet a star like you."

"Did we go to school together?" he said meekly.

Mama, Lanelle, and Dusty assumed by his responses

that he had Alzheimer's. But I sized up the situation and noticed that the legless individual in the wheelchair was a regular-sized person. It dawned on me that we had the wrong man.

I inched out of his room and literally went weak with laughter, leaning on the wall for support. Once I regained my composure, I reentered room 103 and mouthed to Lanelle, "He's not the munchkin. *Not* the munchkin."

Mama was still fawning loudly over the gentleman, so it took Lanelle a moment to relay the message. My mother was smooth, though. While maintaining her decibel level, she eased out and thanked him very much for his time. As we left a nurse divulged the correct address for our munchkin.

We hooted, hollered, and howled when we got in the car. And yes, we did meet the real munchkin that day. His name is Karl Slover, and he was gracious and lovely toward us. We visited him for nearly an hour, and he regaled us with stories about Ray Milland and Judy Garland. He shared a poignant note from his childhood: His father would have men pull his arms and legs for hours on end in hopes of stretching him to make him taller. At the age of twenty-one he stood only two feet and escaped to show business.

As we got up to leave and said our good-byes, Mama put something in his minuscule shirt pocket. It was a carefully folded twenty-dollar bill. At first I was appalled: She had tipped the damn munchkin! But then I considered the spirit in which it was given. She might speak at high volume to certain people, but she also regularly tips beleaguered cooks, janitors, and anyone who looks like he could use a lift. So what if Mr. Slover didn't need the money or a lift. It was still an unabashed act of love.

Jesus and Mammy

Always included in our gallivanting is a visit to a cavernous building with consignment booths offering everything from crocheted toilet-roll covers to pitchforks. But Jesus holds forth here. So does Mammy, the old racial caricature of the African American woman. You know her: the plump, smiling domestic worker in red kerchief and apron. As Aunt Jemima, she's sold millions of pancakes.

This building is the domain of these Southern icons. They are everywhere, in the form of knickknacks and whatnot. Jesus is the bigger commercial draw of the two—his merchandise outsells Mammy's, but she's still a solid commodity.

Shoppers can select from 3-D Jesus paintings, T-shirts, lamps, figurines, wallet cards, clocks, caps, nightlights, and action figures. In addition to the Baby Jesus, you can buy a Biker Jesus or a GI Jesus. My favorite shirt reads LACK OF EXPOSURE TO THE SON CAN CAUSE BURNING.

Mammy, on the other hand, is kept in her place, which is squarely in the kitchen. Her likeness is reproduced on salt-and-pepper shakers, toothpick holders, trivets, resting spoons, bottle openers, dishcloths, sugar and creamer sets, and oodles of cookie jars.

When they lock up the building at night, I bet Jesus and Mammy have some interesting conversations about what they heard that day or the people who kept picking them up but not buying.

"I'd love to see a high-school couple go to the prom dressed as Jesus and Mammy," I say to Mama and Donna. "Wouldn't that just mess everybody up?"

They've become experts at ignoring me when I say such outlandish things, but we're having a ball, so it doesn't matter.

Animals Behaving Oddly

After a few strenuous hours of rambling, my favorite place for lunch is Ma Hawkin's Restaurant. Blue imitation-leather booths, cocola in eight-ounce bottles, and potato salad served with crackers before the meal. Me-Maw denounced Ma Hawkin's as "highfalutin." This simply meant that the patrons were people who put their money in a bank instead of a coffee can. In her mind, "pure-T snobs."

While settling in to eat, I get to hear the latest stories involving peculiar animal behavior. I guess country life is closer to nature, and that's why nature gets so close on occasion.

One nice spring day they propped open the front and back doors of the bank. Before you knew it, a deer clacked right through the front door as if he needed to make a deposit. Tellers and customers started screaming, and the deer leaped over the counter and ran straight out the back door.

Another time a Chihuahua named Pizza went to the Pig like he did every day to meet his friend Miss Raynette Scruggs. (The Pig is what we call the Piggly-Wiggly, a grocery store chain.) Miss Raynette would arrive at the Pig at ten a.m. and give Pizza a homemade biscuit from the pocket of her housedress. On this day, however, she was sick and couldn't get out. Pizza walked into the Pig and looked mournfully around for her. When the cashier saw him, she said, "Go on home now, Pizza. Don't worry—Miss Raynette will be back tomorrow."

As if he understood perfectly, he turned around and trotted home.

Mama, of course, had to then chime in with her own story about One-Eyed Dale. He's her neighbor Lynn's brother.

"Would you believe that this one-eyed man has two one-eyed dogs, too?" says Mama. "One came that way, and the other got that way."

Several weeks prior she and Lynn were sitting on the porch and up walked a one-eyed squirrel. Mama turned slowly toward her neighbor and whispered, "You thinkin' what I'm thinkin'? Let's catch 'im for Dale!"

Mama pounced, but the squirrel eluded capture.

Crime Report

At the end of a day of scooterpootin', I dive into the stack of crime reports Mama has clipped from the newspaper. Compared to Atlanta or Savannah, the reports read like the funny papers. There is almost no serious crime in Dublin. The gravest offense cited might be the heist of a case of Aqua Net hairspray. The delicious combination of content, language, and brevity make for an amusing read.

The following are real excerpts, reproduced in their entirety and exactly as they appeared in the Dublin *Courier Herald*:

- Kenneth Daniel of Dublin reported July 27 he lost a cell phone while riding a tractor.
- A woman reported May 11 a co-worker snatched items from her hand and broke her fingernail.
- An 18-year-old learned on May 17 that his father has used his name and Social Security number to rent an apartment and get telephone service and did not pay the bill.
- A man reported July 30 a young teen drove his golf cart around his house and shot birds at him.
- A man reported on May 13 that his brother stole his dog to sell for drug money. (Mama flagged this one with a note that read, "I like this one.")
- A man reported May 5 he was struck by lightening [sic] while trying to use his ATM card.

- A woman reported June 7 a man she had lived with returned to the home and kicked holes in her juvenile daughter's bedroom walls and urinated on the daughter's bed, clothes, and books.
- Florine Harris reported Aug. 15 that her decal went missing.
- An employee of First American Rental reported a former employee took a camcorder from a vehicle and refuses to return it until a marijuana pipe that was taken from the vehicle he was driving is returned to him.
- An employee of Food Max reported on May 21 that a man stole a wine cooler and drank it in the bathroom.
- A woman reported May 18 another woman assaulted her while a group was watching wrestling and drinking alcohol.
- A woman reported April 27 another woman called her and gave her intimate details that were taking place between the caller and the woman's husband. The woman and her husband are now separated and still the calls continue with the caller threatening to slash her throat and the throats of her tiny children while they sleep.
- A woman reported Oct. 12 she and her husband got into a dispute and he threatened her. The husband said he believes his wife is trying to establish a "paper trail" for the purpose of intending to kill him to collect insurance money and he denies that he even so much as yelled at the wife.

- A man reported May 4 another man threatened him.
- A Georgia Power employee reported May 11 a man became angry over his power bill, cursed them and slammed the door when he left.
- A deputy struck a deer on Oct. 8 but the patrol vehicle was only slightly damaged because of the bumper.

You know you're in a quiet town when it's relaxing to read the crime reports. In contrast, crime in Atlanta is so dreadful that I have to take frequent breaks from reading the papers. And I never watch the local news. The thugs in Atlanta make Savannah's bad guys look like Keystone criminals. In Atlanta they steal ambulances from outside the emergency room; they murder a single mom for the food in her fridge and a bag of diapers; they prostitute eleven-year-olds; and they pull a truck driver out of his truck, almost killing him just for the hell of it. It's petrifying.

I much prefer to be scared by a good horror tale or something I've cooked up in my mind. My imagination is greedy and demands frequent feedings. Only on trips home do I find stories and experiences that satisfy my ravenous brain.

We Mean You No Harm

*M*ama's half sister Lanelle was born with the veil—a membrane that surrounds the fetus and occasionally covers the head at birth. It is said that those born with the veil have second sight. Sure enough, Lanelle sees horrendous things before they happen, and folks seek her help in discerning their dreams. When she joined us for a day of ghost hunting, I knew she'd intensify the whole endeavor.

My then nineteen-year-old nephew Dusty had been telling me about "haunted" locations around Dublin and wanted me to come visit and go looking for spirits with him. I desperately needed a break from metro Atlanta anyway. And this was not the kind of adventure I'd ever find in the big city.

His tales were a bit fantastic—stories about everything from a dilapidated funeral home that shook to one about being chased by a hobgoblin that threw marbles at him. I didn't actually expect any encounters with spectral beings, especially during daylight hours. I figured we'd have a fun time and that Lanelle would lend harmless occult drama to the proceedings.

WRONG.

Our first stop was the Bell Brown Home, an abandoned nursing home well-known in the area to bored teenagers looking for late-night fright. To enter the property you have to drive under a decrepit arched iron sign. Some letters on the sign have fallen off, parts of others dangle and creak in the winter wind.

It makes for an unnerving greeting. Lanelle, Dusty, and I simultaneously gave one another a look, as if to say, "Uh-oh. This place is freaky. What are we getting ourselves into?"

Lanelle's expression confirmed that we were about to meet some real live haints. It was in her eyes: First she made them big and then squinted in pain. She held the squint for an awfully long while. It seems she's always being tortured by knowledge that folks aren't meant to have.

Jeepers creepers, where did she get those peepers? Her look could put Bela Lugosi to shame. Make Nosferatu run crying for his mummy. She gave me a serious case of the heebie-jeebies.

She can't help it. It's in her genes, and she considers it a scourge. Her paternal grandmother was a known witch who was observed incanting over rats before swinging them, by their tails, into the fire. I'm not related to the witch—her son was the man my grandmother Me-Maw ran off with to Florida. I think Lanelle got a double dose of granny's juju, because her premonitions have been coming true for decades. When her brother Scooter was injured in a serious car wreck, Lanelle saw every detail the night before and tried to warn him. She's also made many accurate predictions about illnesses and unexpected demises. We trust her completely. If she said werewolves were living in a catacomb under my house, I'd go straight to the store for silver bullets.

As a young teen, I looked forward to spending weekends with her in River Wall. Something scary happened every time: black mists in her bedroom, a message scrawled on the bathroom mirror, objects moving. During one visit, she felt that her husband had been hurt and said we'd hear the ambulance siren in a moment. The siren came less than one minute later. Then a friend called to tell her he'd been in a minor car accident. That was a normal day for her.

Lanelle never envisions anything positive, never sees winning lottery numbers, cancer remissions, or who'll win the Super Bowl. Instead, it's unrelenting bad news. She would gladly give up her ability, but can't. My aunt is no witch, just a beautiful loving soul with a direct pipeline to the dark side.

We braced ourselves for what lay inside the Bell Brown Home—everybody except Mama, that is. Drawing on her billionth cigarette, she said we shouldn't be trespassing and that she'd stay in the car for when the police were called on us. She was clearly aggravated by the entire shenanigans. We begged and pleaded with her to go in with us—until she shot us her look—the You're About to Snap My Last Good Nerve and I Won't Be

Responsible for What Happens Next look. At which point we shut up and got out of the car.

The back door of the nursing home was wide open. The three of us approached it as if it was Satan's Express Elevator to Eternal Damnation. But we were excited, too, and loving every edgy minute. It was perverse entertainment, on the verge of going wrong.

We stuck so close to one another that I could feel Lanelle's heart pounding. It is not a good sign when the Head Soothsayer is nutting up. And how was it that they had slipped behind me so that I was in front?

Realizing how silly we were being, I led us inside. Within two seconds a window slammed and crashed. Now we were scared out of our skulls and only three feet inside the door. We pressed on anyway.

The back part of the place was the eeriest. It was a large room filled with a long row of twin beds set close together. One could imagine the old and dying languishing there, stick figures calling out in pain and confusion. Many of the beds were still perfectly made despite a caved-in roof and years of plunder. A pair of dentures was intentionally set out at the foot of one bed—dentures that looked like they belonged to Paul Lynde. They smiled and mocked us. In the corner was evidence of a squatter.

Lanelle was overcome with the sadness all around her, her eyes filling with water. "Do you feel that?" she asked. "There's definitely something here." Dusty's eyes had become glazed, as if he'd been overtaken by something. The atmosphere was charged, crackling with the residual emotions and suffering of its former residents.

The legend is that everyone left the Bell Brown Home in the middle of the night, just up and left their belongings and vanished. As we walked through the other rooms, I could see why people thought that.

Clothes still hung in the closets, a man's wallet—complete with ID cards—was on a table, and piles of business checks written by Ms. Bell Brown herself were strewn across a floor. Things didn't add up. A decapitated baby doll head with one eyelid down . . . a single cowboy boot standing at attention in a doorway. One shoe, whether boot, slipper, or Manolo Blahnik, is always a terrible omen.

Dusty said there were dead people—well, photos of dead people—in the kitchen, but they were not there on that day, thank goodness. He was probably talking about funeral pictures. Some rural Southerners treasure photos of their deceased loved ones. When Me-Maw died, Mama took rolls of film of her in the casket. At least twenty close-ups of her face alone.

The longer we poked around the nursing home, the weirder it got. The skies were lonesome gray, but the contents of the rooms were bathed in panic color—an unnatural cast you see when your brain goes kaflooey, similar to when things switch into slow motion when you're in shock.

Lanelle reported that presences were everywhere, shaking her head at things only she could see. The

Scourge of the Veil. As if on cue, Dusty descended into catatonia, and I announced that it was time to leave.

Despite Dusty's condition, he managed to leap into the car faster than a jackrabbit on crack. We all did. Mama, still worried that we were going to get caught, stomped the gas pedal hard enough to burn rubber and jerk our necks.

Lanelle and I started telling her about our experiences. "We have to go back so that you can see what we're talking about," implored Lanelle.

"Yeah, Mama—you won't believe it. It's wild in there. Come on—you'd actually enjoy it."

Mama restated her position against trespassing but concurred that she would enjoy seeing the home.

"But not for the reasons you think. I would like to look around just because it would be interesting— fascinating to see what's there. And I'm *not* talking about ghosts, either. I hate to tell you this, but y'all just got worked up over a whole bunch of nothin'—you hear me? And if you're smart, you'll quit worrying me about going back there. I'd like to see it one day but not without the owner's permission. And that's the end of that."

Before going to our next supernatural location, we went to a Mexican restaurant to have lunch and decompress. I was concerned about Dusty: His dull gaze was fixed on something above my head—had he been spirited away? Turned into a changeling? Or was he staring at an entity floating around up there? Just as I was wondering how to look up an exorcist in the phone book,

I saw what was capturing his attention: a hot-oil bikini contest on the wall-mounted TV behind me.

During lunch Aunt Lanelle told us that she's had a vision of a gruesome car accident happening in front of her house. She's seen smoking wreckage and blood-drenched victims laid out in her yard and is just waiting for it to occur. It hasn't happened yet, but we know it will. Dusty claimed that our next destination was an old funeral home where coffins were stacked on the front porch. Admittedly, Southerners have used their porches in some funky ways, but I was keen to debunk this outrageous story. He had to be mistaken, didn't he?

Mama got nervous again when she realized that the funeral home sat on a remote piece of private property plastered with No Trespassing signs. Dusty assured her that it was not far down the dirt road, but it turned out to be not close, either. And it was perfectly hidden in an outcropping of trees and overgrowth. You'd have to know what you were looking for to even find it.

As we got closer, I could determine that it was a farmhouse from the late 1800s. In ruins—the floors no longer existed, but the outline of the structure was intact. Tenacious webs of kudzu enveloped it and held it together. The scene was pure, undisturbed Southern Gothic. Then we spied the big boxes on the porch.

"See, I told you," says Dusty like a man vindicated. "Look right there."

He pointed out the name on one of the boxes: Pvt. Herman N. Cooper. Above the name was stamped:

HADLEY FUNERAL HOME. There were other such boxes on the porch as well. They must have been used to ship home the bodies of servicemen. I explained to Dusty that they weren't coffins but the containers that held them. Despite the sight of death containers and a funeral home straight out of a Rob Zombie flick, this place had none of the foreboding of the Bell Brown Home. It was completely void of shadows—and a little bit of a letdown.

By the time we left the farmhouse, it was getting late and there was only one thing to do before going home: return to Bell Brown with Mama.

We started in on her, nagging and needling her to join us inside Dublin's most bone-chilling, ghost-infested hellhole. She got so agitated that she veered into oncoming traffic and nearly took out a construction barrel. Pulling over to regroup, she lit the billionth-and-sixth cigarette and made an announcement.

"All right, by God—we're going to the fuckin' Bell Brown Home. In the meantime, don't anybody say another damn word to me about it."

And with that she floorboarded it and whiplashed us all the way there.

"Before we go in," she said, "I have just one question: Why exactly are we lookin' for something that we don't want to find?"—dramatic pause—"No, seriously, can someone please tell me why we are hunting ghosts when we hope to God we don't catch any?"

Mama, ever the pithy observer, made us bust out

laughing. Then she led the expedition inside in her usual no-nonsense manner.

She began by belting out, "Hello—Hello—if anyone is here, we mean you no harm.... We mean you no harm!"

With a voice that can strip paint off steel girders, Mama must have thought the phantoms were hard of hearing. The screeching of WE MEAN YOU NO HARM continued although she occasionally alternated it with a pleasant sing-song version: *We mean you no haaa-aarm, haaa-aarm.*

Apparently it banished the evil forces because I noticed that birds were singing again and the panic color had drained out of everything. Mama strolled through the rooms like she was at an exhibit.

"Oh, look at that doll's head over there—I bet it was a comfort to someone here. . . . Now, that's a shame that the mate for this cowboy boot is missing because somebody would give five dollars easy for those boots at the flea market—they're nice boots. . . ."

On and on she went, interpreting the home and its contents with clear eyes and total fearlessness.

We were baffled at how different the place was this time. Mama, who is a match for any haint, made us see Bell Brown as it really was instead of how our imaginations made it.

"Honey, the dead ones can't do anything to you," she said. "It's the live ones you have to worry about."

Aunt Lanelle might have second sight, but Mama has a special talent for seeing things.

When the day was over, Lanelle got me juiced up again with a story about a ghastly experience she had one night. Right after lying down, she became paralyzed, unable to move or speak for five minutes. Later a coworker explained to her that a witch must have been "riding" her, and that's why she was immobilized. The coworker told her to open her Bible to John 3:10 and place it under the bed for protection.

I was enthralled by the story and hanging on every word, but Mama wasn't particularly moved.

She just took a drag off the billionth-and-ninth cigarette and purred, "I can't say I've ever been rode by a witch, but I have been ridden by some real sons of bitches."

Artifice

The world of today is sick to its thin blood
for lack of elemental things, for fire before
the hands, for water welling from the earth,
for air, for the dear earth underfoot.

—FROM *The Outermost House* BY HENRY BESTON

I had been on the commute home from work for two hours but had gone only twenty-three miles. An accident had immobilized the roadways. As I sat in the stalled traffic, with eighteen-wheelers idling around me, I grumbled, "This is no way to live."

Then a man toting a cane fishing pole walked by the car. He wore overalls and had a bait bucket in the other hand. I was absolutely euphoric. In the midst of all the congestion and frustration, here was a reminder that some part of the old world still existed. The new rules say that a man should not be walking on a major road. Roads are for cars and trucks and commerce. And cancer fumes and rage and wrecks. Yet he was there: a picture of rural simplicity and groundedness.

I live in the suburbs and work in Atlanta, the city that has the unhealthiest commute in the country. I've found that spending so much time in transit complicates the simplest things and disconnects one from the meaningful. It imposes such an unnatural way of life that the vision of a fisherman will make you lose your mind. Goats and the sound of a rooster's crow have the same effect. They jolt you back and tell you that sprawl has not strangled everything, despite seas of concrete, blacktop, wrecking balls, pylons, and other man-made garbage that you navigate around daily.

But within a few seconds you're right back where you were—reacting without thinking. Lurching two steps backward for every fumble forward. Permanent retrograde. And you don't have to be a commuter to be asleep at the wheel of your life. It's just what caused my affliction. I never thought I'd succumb to such a state— that I'd drift so far away from being a Cracker Queen. I let seven years of commuting obliterate all the work I'd begun at Pinkie's.

While watching the fisherman disappear into the nearby woods, the scene struck me as a metaphor not just for me but for my town of Powder Springs. It's a bedroom community that has seen rapid residential growth at the expense of its small-town charm. Old-timers recall large swaths of farmland and forests where treeless subdivisions now reign.

Like me, many of the subdivision people leave early for work in Atlanta and come home late. It's dark outside when we pull out of our driveways and pitch-black when we return. Some years I miss the blooming of my camellias because I haven't seen the yard in the light of day, not on most weekdays anyway. If I arrive in time to hear the Methodist church carillon, I'm ecstatic because it means I've made it home by six p.m.

When I moved to Powder Springs, I became a community volunteer so that I would have roots. My involvement has been rewarding beyond what I imagined, but it has also made me aware that the town's distinctive elements are eroding. Bug Porter's business is one of them.

For more than fifty years, codgers have gathered at Bug's lawn mower sales and service business. They sit outside on cracked vinyl chairs and crack on the people and cars that go by on Main Street. It's the headquarters for gossip and tall tales, and women are not welcome, which is fine with me. I don't want to integrate, I just like to catch a glance of them when I pass by.

A road project will soon dislocate the business. The same project that will erase the Flat, the town's old African American neighborhood and turn my street into a major thoroughfare. All of this after the demolition of the one remaining historic public building—a two-story school that was leveled to make way for a library. At least it is a library. They designed it in a 1920s style, but it's about as authentic-looking as Joan Rivers. After years of the commuting life, I don't even feel that authentic.

Instead of protecting the things that give our place

character and cohesion, we've splintered and become like every other suburban nightmare. It's the curse of identical details: same fast food establishments, chain stores, restaurants; same perceptions, decisions, actions. The town mirrors the homogeny and monotony of our treadmill existence. It parallels our dullness.

After a while I started jonesing for some of the color of life in Savannah—a hint of hoodoo, perhaps; maybe just one geriatric vigilante—or how about a kid I could overpay to cut my grass poorly? No, not here. In pursuing the so-called American Dream, I'd priced myself out of the market I really wanted to live in. I missed the screwballs and crack-ups.

Powder Springs is deteriorating because the commuters have no attachment to it. Our lives are frenetic and superficial. We're constantly racing against the clock, even as we're stopped dead in traffic. A mentality develops, one that focuses on rushing and buying things instead of getting rid of them. Buying and consuming offer quick gratification but don't fill us up. A mindlessness sets in. Rather than taking a walk in the neighborhood, we purchase overpriced and unnecessary bike gear, load it on our SUVs, and lug it to a crowded public trail for exercise. We are completely distracted and separated from what makes us alive. These sick behaviors beget actual illness, and then we wonder what in the world made us sick.

I'll tell you what else has made us puny: a turning away from adventure, risk, community, nonconformity, and creativity. The typical suburban commuter doesn't really know his neighbors. He has a security system in his home and would like to see more security lights on his street. Security is just a code word for fear. It's interesting that fear runs amok in the places people flock to for safety.

I admit that we had security systems in Savannah, but they were better known as shotguns and semi-automatics. I prefer to shoot out the lights so that I can admire the stars. And doesn't one have to *be* in darkness to see the light?

When I'm running errands around town, I will drive miles out of my way just so I can lay eyes on the goats, an old barn, or laundry drying on a line. I know where to find all the remnants because I've scoped them out. They are essential to my sanity. Occasionally, on a holiday or a quiet Sunday evening, I'll trek out to a road that makes me feel that I'm almost in the country. The rolling hills are dotted with farms and lopsided outbuildings and modest houses; there's even a pasture with burros. But keep going and the landscape becomes blighted by McMansions: dung palaces of excess and subpar construction. Pardon me if that sounds like the rantings of a Communist dictator, but I'd rather cozy up to Fidel than be at the mall all weekend.

The McMansions line up side-by-side like soldiers in formation on parched, conquered land. The developments market themselves with ludicrous names such as The Reserve at Monastery Lakes or Village Pointe Vineyard Estates. The tagline should read "Oversized status homes for underutilized minds." This road eventually empties into a highway of endless shopping centers.

Although many independent establishments have faded away, one is still going strong: Bailey's Family Restaurant. Located close to my house, it's a reassuring icon. Elvis and Santa Claus eat there. So do the old, the infirm, the workers, the dreamers, the Baptists and the Methodists, and the misfits.

We all go there because everyone is genuinely loved there. The owners, Theresa, Zack, and Peter, see to it personally. If medical expenses devastate a local family, Bailey's holds fund-raising dinners. At Christmas they give a festive party for hundreds of folks who might otherwise be alone or without cheer during the holidays. Kids in attendance receive toys and visit with Santa. Senior citizens are presented gift bags and tap their toes to performances by "Elvis" or a duo with the unsexy stage name of Bill and Mary. The only hitch is that the guests don't want to leave.

When I am at Bailey's, it's as if I've traveled to a different time and place—it's real community and an antidote after the long commute home. There are bright spots and creative people doing things in Powder Springs, but the grind of the commuting life keeps us from them.

I think the town is like a pudgy twelve-year-old girl who can't decide if she wants to stay small or grow up. Her hormones are out of whack and she yearns to turn back but can't. She's in the middle, in limbo. Between worlds, just like me. I'm caught too, between a job I love and a commute that is exacting a mighty price on my wellness.

I have chosen these circumstances, but the glorious bit is that I can choose something else. Didn't I supposedly learn that way back when I observed Aunt Martha in action? And what has taken me so long to see that a different choice is needed? It should have raised a flag when I found myself following the herd, doing what everyone else was doing. I have never been a herd girl.

I didn't question it because there weren't enough hours in the day for contemplation or evaluation—not when I had to go get gas for the second time that week, grab takeout on the way home, run to a meeting, and then plop into bed. And what happened to the fun? I bought a hula-hoop for my office but barely used it.

Going through the motions for so long has made me forget some of the most essential lessons I ever learned. Only after I started remembering them did I see what I'd actually lost: time to dream, relationships, a sense of my authentic self. The soul of my town is being sacrificed for the same reason: We're suffering from amnesia when it comes to the shared values that bind a community. And we're blind to what's slipping away.

The most chilling aspect of a life lived by default is the self-deception. Ask us and we'll tell you we're living the high life. In truth it is killing us. To be authentic you have to first be honest with yourself. I finally realized that if I didn't start acting like a Cracker Queen, I'd perish on the vine.

Not long ago nine people died in one day in unrelated car accidents during the commute. Funny how that sort of news is rarely reported. When Atlanta was named the worst commuting city by Forbes.com, the ranking was based on statistics such as the number of fatalities and fine particulates in the air.

I have decided that change is now in the air for me. I won't be moving into a teepee and renouncing the world anytime soon. I like running water and electricity too much, not to mention bubble baths, French fries, and twenty-one-dollar lipstick. But the world I inhabit is going to be different because I am shucking the curse of identical details.

Fuck conformity. I am a Cracker Queen. We throw cigarettes to the chain gang.

Fuck security. We stare down Dog Fighters. We roam the worst streets of London in an effort to serve others.

Fuck smallness. Our love and expression of life is extreme and large and loud. Therefore, this bullshit is about to change. I have embarked on a plan based on the core values I'd written down on the cocktail napkins at Pinkie's. I've expanded the list and mulled over the changes I have to make.

I will quit my job. Despite the satisfaction of the work, it is the cause of the commute, and it's got to go. I will make time for the things that move me and give me joy. When I saw the fisherman on the side of the road that day, I understood the depth of my loss and vowed to reclaim my crown.

Designing my new life has been beyond thrilling. The mystery and adventure are back. So are the belly laughs. Everything is better and getting more so. I am clearing the decks and becoming myself again. It might have been safe in the suburbs, but the riches are still in the sea. I'm taking the dive. And I will not turn back.

My engagement in this culture of artifice is coming to an end. The spell is broken and I'm awake. I will lighten my load and live like the fisherman: simply and with imagination. I will follow the ways of the Cracker Queen.

Part Three

The Way of the Cracker Queen

Living Out Loud, Laughing Hard, and Loving Life to Death

The Regal Essentials

*T*hese are the linchpins of the Cracker Queen world. Without them we're just mean ol' white trash—the unhappiest and most havoc-wreaking creatures in the whole trailer park. Crazy Aunt Carrie comes immediately to mind.

Love

Love is pure magic. And the mojo of love is limitless. It cannot be contained, chained, bossed, or bowed. It is Lord of All. In its presence cups overflow and fear disintegrates. Love for the sake of love is the highest state and should be our constant aspiration. We might come to its altar in tube tops and flip-flops, and sometimes with a note from our parole officer, but we worship nonetheless.

Cracker Queens understand that any problem can be tackled if we approach it from a place of love. When a CQ whups someone's ass, it's because the person requires a jolt that cannot be administered any other way. A CQ wouldn't bother with the person if she didn't love him. Seriously, we get nowhere unless we love one another. It is the Supreme Law. This I know more than anything else.

Forgiveness

Everyone has been hurt. Everyone has been done wrong. Even Queens get royally screwed. . . . Get over it! Regardless of your story, you must let go of the anger and forgive. Notice I didn't say to forget—that would be downright foolish, like inviting the scoundrel back in for more bologna sandwiches and pork rinds.

Nothing releases you like forgiveness. It unlocks the most self-destructive mind-set and in turn sets you free. It's the ultimate disinfectant, dissolving negative mental energy on contact. The keys to forgiveness will be handed to you when you work to become more loving.

Grudges, whether large or small, aren't just pointless— they're menacing bloodsuckers that keep you under the spell of the one who's hurt you. Grudges suspend you in the amber of someone else's making. Why would you hand over your power like that?

I know it's not as easy as just saying "poof" and making the grudges disappear. It's often hard, long work, but the rewards of having an open heart make it well worth it. Despite a rocky childhood, I hold no grudge against my mother. I could easily focus on the ragged ghosts of thirty years ago, but driving a car stuck in reverse is not my idea of fun.

Gratitude

Gratitude is the cherry on top of the ice-cream sundae or the big bow on top of your dream car. It brings an extra sweetness to everything.

Regardless of what gets thrown at me, I strive to view it through a lens of gratitude. I ask what kind of gift or lesson is hidden within the disaster. What good can come from it? Being grateful can change a situation from one that would set you back to one that will catapult you forward. I learned this when my daddy died.

When I was growing up we stayed flat broke. The purchase of a poster board for school was cause for wailing and gnashing of teeth. Going out to eat was the wildest luxury. To this day I revel in dining out, buying office supplies, and doing the other activities that were not possible back then. There's no bitterness, just joy.

If you're depressed, list the things for which you're grateful and then think about each one. It sounds hackneyed, but have you tried it? This exercise will help you be less despondent and more balanced in your assessment of things. And when we get to the point of being in a state of ongoing thanksgiving, it seems to alter our brain chemistry. Something shifts radically. Something that influences everything else in a positive way.

A palm reader once took a glance at my hand and said, "Good Lord, you have had one rough life."

I was taken aback—I don't think about it that way. I actually had to stop and consider it for a moment. That's because I give thanks for all kinds of things at all times: from Daddy going to the grave without ever hearing the "jazz" of Kenny G—to living within earshot of a train whistle.

Mama, who you've probably figured out is the Queen of All Cracker Queens, knows about being appreciative. I was visiting her recently when she complained that the only physical reminder she had of Daddy was a dented cake pan from their marriage.

"Are you sure that's all you have?" I asked.

"No, on second thought, I do have something else," she said. "I have all those lovely memories."

She spoke it without a trace of sarcasm. Remarkable when you recall some of the lowlights of their years together. Extraordinary when you consider that the cake pan probably got dented over one of their heads during a hellacious fight. It took her a while to get there, but love and forgiveness nudged her along.

Purpose: Gotta Have It

Queen Ella Fitzgerald sang, "It don't mean a thing if it ain't got that swing." Likewise, we cannot attain Queendom until we identify with the higher source of power both around us and inside us. I would call it God, but I don't want to lose anyone.

It starts in the act of remembering our spiritual roots, our closeness to the divine. It's the spark that makes all the darkness in the world unable to snuff out the light of one candle. We are all members of the great body of light. It is when we forget who we are that the darkness creeps in—any number of emotions that over time cause us to die little deaths.

Like everyone else, I have had some tumultuous trials. I couldn't have overcome them by smarts and a strong will alone. I had to call on something deeper, something that is within me but transcended the power of me. The part that remains when we strip away the physical body and mind and their limitations.

As we remember our true natures, we see a purpose in our lives that is beyond the pursuit of the material. Don't get me wrong: I agree with George Bernard Shaw that lack of money is the root of all evil. Or as Mama says, "Money isn't everything, but it sure quiets the nerves."

The acquisition of money is necessary and wise, but it shouldn't be our sole aim. Just as an obsession with looking younger or climbing professional ladders will leave you unfulfilled, attachment to worldly things separates you from what matters most.

When the authentic self reveals itself, it tells us that we're here to serve others. The particular manner in which we serve is what gives us our authenticity. I come from a long line of women who understood authenticity and service.

My great-great-aunt Minnie was a suffragette who fought for equality when it was most unfashionable. One of my most treasured possessions is the beaded purse she carried in marches and into jail cells. My great-aunt

Martha, as president of the Hartford, Connecticut, school board, worked to make things better for several generations of students. And my aunt Ellie devoted her entire life to causes of social justice and spiritual development. She participated in the historic March on Washington and volunteered for years as the associate pastor of the Washington, DC, city jail. At the age of seventy-eight, she edited a textbook urging radical reform of the criminal justice system.

I gasped when she gave me her souvenir button from the March on Washington; I understood the responsibility implicit in receiving the gift.

Not all of us have to be activists and reformers, but we can be great only if we serve.

Put Your Fist into Fear

> I dried my tears, and arm'd my fears
> With ten thousand shields and spears.
>
> —FROM "The Angel" BY WILLIAM BLAKE

Like moonshine made in a radiator, fear kills. That's why you have to put your fist into it first. Otherwise it will destroy every possibility of moving forward. Fears feed on you until nothing is left but a bony carcass. Again, Crazy Aunt Carrie is a good figurative and literal example of this. Bless her blackened, shriveled heart.

As we catch glimpses of our authentic selves, we have less and less fear because we see past the worries of the physical world, the inauthentic realm. We see that we are fine and will continue to be OK. That we are enough and we have enough.

So why do we allow ourselves to live a miserable existence infused with and informed by fear? Well, of course you know the answer: Staring down a fear just seems too daunting. It feels more comfortable and safe to maintain the world you've known. To face the fear would be to eliminate it, and then what would we do? We decide it's far too much to take on, so we retreat. And if you're a slow learner like me, maybe it takes some time to believe in what's authentic.

I've had glimmers of my authentic self as long as I can remember, but fear was always loitering nearby, jerking the curtains back in place so I couldn't see. Never underestimate fear's power; he's one persistent, pernicious mutha.

For nearly twenty years I was scared shitless about making a serious attempt at a writing career. Even though I knew deep down that I was meant to do it, I contrived every excuse in the book as to why I shouldn't.

Here's a small sampling of my excuses:

1. I have a day job and don't have time to write.
2. I will fail.
3. I will fail in spectacular fashion and end up destitute.
4. Once destitute, I will become homeless and go insane as a result of having my dream destroyed.

The Cracker Queen 183

5. Even if I don't become a crazy bag lady, I'll still need a writing room, and I can't afford to build or buy one. If only I had a special place in which to write . . .

6. I'm a crap writer anyway.

7. Why bother when the immortal poets and writers have produced such luminous work?

8. Everybody wants to be a writer. What makes me think I could make it?

9. The odds of finding an agent and getting a book deal are slimmer than nil.

10. I shouldn't be wasting my time and energy on something that will never happen.

11. Writing will have to be a hobby because I must keep my secure day job in order to survive. I don't have any other option. I should go back to graduate school and pursue a safe career goal.

As you see, I was firmly in fear's clutches, to the point of irrational thinking and major delusion. My reptilian brain, the area that houses the fight-or-flight mechanism, was the size of an anaconda and kept me fleeing. This fear denies access to the feast of life. Nothing is sadder than that.

"Do one thing every day that scares you." I keep this quote from Eleanor Roosevelt on my desk. Each time I follow Mrs. Roosevelt's advice, I am made stronger and less afraid of the next thing. It has a cascading effect, because boldness itself generates momentum that turbocharges your life in the right direction.

Go gunning for whatever frightens you. Take it head-on. That's the surefire way to get unstuck. When I first made the leap and started writing seriously, I felt like a fool, like I'd put my neck on the chopping block. Instead of losing my head, I gained my freedom. And now Dear Reader, you hold my book in your hand.

One final caveat: I acknowledge that some fears are prudent, such as fears of bears in the wild, cigarettes lit next to oxygen tanks, and Lynyrd Skynyrd cover bands.

Two Billion Heartbeats

I'm an optimist, but not the annoying kind. One of those was ahead of me in jaw-clenching traffic once and had a bumper sticker that read, OPTIMISM—A GREAT WAY OF LIFE!

The nerve! I'd like to see his optimism when I rear-end his ass, I thought. Somebody should slash his tires for that, I grumbled out loud. As mean as the world is, and he's riding around advocating optimism! He'd better be careful where he parks that thing. Somebody's liable to hurl a brick through the windshield, and it might be me!

Sorry, but mindless cheeriness leaves a bad taste in my mouth. I'll never say, "When life gives you lemons, make lemonade," or "Don't sweat the small stuff." Who am I to say your stuff is small? It just doesn't work like that.

My optimism lies in what some would deem a depressing truth: All things go away. Knowing that everything, good and bad, will pass has enabled me to live in the moment, with joy and humor. The poet Elizabeth Bishop called it the "art of losing." This notion has made me an optimist for the real world, with all its suffering, ugliness, and pain. The fact that things fall apart, or die, is not depressing to me, for I see it as the most natural phenomenon, an organic cycle.

The understanding of the temporality of life grounds me—it brings the assurance that hard times will evaporate one day and be replaced with something new. That hope sustains me and forces me to move on. And it softens the blow when good times come to an end. This gritty optimism anchors my life. The people I've admired most are those who've lost everything but are still able to see the splendid possibilities ahead.

Several times a week I take walks through a cemetery. I'm usually listening to music that gets me energized and dancing among the headstones. I love the thought of being joyful in a place associated with sadness.

Similarly, for Halloween I decorate plastic skeletons by putting pink tutus around their waists and hanging them at different levels from the front porch. They twist and turn in the wind, appearing to be leaping and cavorting happily. Humor can strip the spookiest things of their spook.

When you're aware that all things go away, you take nothing for granted and acknowledge the urgency of living. Right *now*. Indeed, now is all we have. There's no time to lollygag. Even if you live to be one hundred, this very instant may be your only chance with the person standing before you.

Every creature, whether human, buzzard, catfish, or lightning bug, has about two billion heartbeats to spend in a lifetime. Time is short. Put tutus on your skeletons. Dance in the cemetery.

The Royal Necessities

Abundance

> Life could be limitless joy, if we would only take it
> for what it is, the way it is given to us.
>
> —LEO TOLSTOY

When I was a kid, Mama told me that I could do anything I set my mind to. I was skeptical. After all, if it was true it meant that the people around me had the same ability. But they never got ahead. I wanted to believe Mama, but our circumstances indicated otherwise.

In retrospect, I received a great education in how to limp along in life, bypassing the proverbial banquet entirely. Before Great-Aunt Martha showed me another way, I dreamed timid, scattershot dreams. I thought the world was out to get me, so I prepared for disappointment and failure. It never occurred to me that perhaps my mental energy was attracting like energy.

I confess to this so that you might believe what I now know:

LIFE IS GIVEN FOR JOY.

We're not supposed to struggle all the time. I had distorted the cosmic picture.

In fact, the Universe is generous, so generous it surpasses human imagination. And we should expect the good because it wants to be found. Tell the Universe what you want, and work like crazy for it. It will come. Ask it for guidance and then shut up and listen.

I guess the banquet actually resembles an all-night diner: It never closes and is open to everyone. Who knew? I certainly didn't. When I walked past that diner, I saw only cracks in the sidewalk and a sign that read Closed.

Acceptance

> Every trial endured and weathered in the right spirit makes a soul nobler and stronger than it was before.
>
> —William Butler Yeats

No matter how beneficent the Universe, pain and hardship will still come a-calling. A Cracker Queen's talent is in turning the bad stuff into usable stuff. She does it by accepting the pain straight-up, just as it is, rather than trying to cover it up or outrun it.

When hit by tragedy, we're not broken. We might be angry for a while—for that which doesn't kill us really pisses us off. But then we're made better. A Cracker Queen doesn't hide from darkness; she tells it to come on in so she can get it over with. She advances through it honestly.

The caterpillar turns into a soupy mess before morphing into a moth. In other words, metamorphosis requires trauma. In suffering, the deepest truths are unmasked. It still sucks, but it pays off in the end.

Me-Maw had a curious saying that went, "Root hog or die!" When I asked Mama what it meant, she explained, "Everyone has to root around in the mud and work in order to survive the hard times. You just have to accept it and do the work."

Humor

If it has tires or testicles, it's gonna give you trouble.

—SAYING POSTED ON MAMA'S FRIDGE

Humor is deadly serious business. It helps us through the darkness better than hard liquor and a carton of menthol lights. The more dire the situation, the bigger joke a Cracker Queen will make about it. And we don't just laugh: We cackle, usually quite inappropriately.

When life is hard, we roar even harder because it's healing. Forget antibiotics, wounds respond best to humor. Another reason we laugh so freely and often is because it's a declaration of love and acceptance.

Trust me, she who laughs, lasts.

Walking Rainbows

If you don't remember anything else, make note of this critical cornerstone of Cracker Queen belief:

EMBELLISHMENT IS A NECESSARY
ADDITION TO EVERYTHING.

We are flashy, outrageous, audacious, and ostentatious. In this respect (and every other), Dolly Parton is one whoppin' Queen. Life is short, so why be tasteful?

It appears that the inclination toward tacky dress is part of our Cracker Queen heritage, as seen in an excerpt from an 1891 magazine article titled "The Georgia Cracker in the Cotton Mills." It reads:

> The inborn taste for color breaks out in flaring ribbons, variegated handkerchiefs, and startling vivid raiment visible miles away, ill-made, ill-fitting, of cheap texture, and loaded with tawdry trimmings, from which the eye turns with relief . . .

The description continues in another passage, pointing out that the Crackers wear "satin shoes for the dusty highways, and costumes of indescribable hues. It is pathetic to see this ignorant groping for beauty in their hard and colorless lives. In lieu of pretty homes and bright possessions, the women make themselves a walking rainbow."

A Yankee gentleman must have authored that article. No one else could have gotten it so wrong. He mistakenly viewed the women through a lens of pity and repulsion. Satin shoes are hopeful things. Flaring ribbons are flags of life. Walking rainbows are, well, walking rainbows! As long as we're in the world, we will live out loud and be the brightest beings around.

Adjust That Crown, Your Horns Are Showing

Not Giving a Damn

I am a Southern girl. We have mud on our feet.

—Tina Turner

By now this will not come as a surprise: To be a Cracker Queen, you cannot give a tinker's damn about what others think. To do so would impede your freedom and authenticity. And that simply will not do.

On September 13, 2001, the first day commercial air travel resumed after the terrorist attacks, I boarded a flight to Amsterdam to visit a friend there. Knowing that Amsterdam had a sizable Muslim immigrant population and ties to cells in nearby Germany, I set out to do something politically incorrect and abhorrent: racial and religious profiling.

I walked the entire length of the plane and eyeballed every passenger, hunting for bulging burkas or sneakers that ticked. I decided that if anyone gave me an uncomfortable feeling, I would bail while there was still time. My walk-through might have caused some uneasiness, as

I didn't conceal what I was doing. But I will remain forever unrepentant because I was protecting myself against an enemy that was vivid and fresh in our psyches at the time. Cracker Queens refuse to be easy prey.

It's fair to say that I am a contrarian when it comes to many things. I hate stuffed animals, think expensive jewelry is a racket, and find little kids utterly uninteresting. I can't stand the sight of school buses; they're egg-yolk-yellow reminders of all the indiscriminate breeding going on.

In the political arena, I can be quite liberal, but I'm right there with the late Charlton Heston when it comes to guns. For most of my life I was terrified of firearms and held them in snobbish contempt. When I realized that my views were based in fear, I stepped out to see what it was about. After a day at the firing range, and with skilled instruction in the care, handling, and shooting of all kinds of guns, I became a convert. My fear was replaced by empowerment. Hell, yeah!

When I enthuse about guns and gun rights, my liberal friends recoil in disbelief. And that is just fine. Cracker Queens live and let live and demand the same in return.

We do not go along with what the media- and marketing-drenched culture wants us to think. We do not exist to please others or to do their bidding. We are our own people, and glorious specimens we are. Because we don't fashion ourselves after anybody else's rules, some say we're off-kilter, off-putting, or just off our rockers. It's perfectly OK if they don't like it—remember, we truly don't give a damn. We rejoice in our difference. And we'll choose self-knowledge over social approval any ol' day.

Victims Ain't Us

> When I was a baby, Daddy used to say that I was the prettiest little thing but that I was a biter.
> —TAMMY, A WAITRESS AT THE WAFFLE HOUSE

All Cracker Queens are biters. Meaning that if you victimize us, we don't stay victims for long. Try and perpetrate on us a second time, and the men in fedoras might be drawing a chalk line around your sorry lifeless body. Attempting to hold a Cracker Queen down is like milking a rattlesnake: It's best not to try it.

Our sense of self-worth is such that victimhood is an insult. Likewise, we do not make excuses, blame our failures on others, or hold pity parties. EVER. If you start whining, we'll tell you faster than a New York minute to SHUT THE HELL UP!

Cracker Queens are disproportionately represented in the noble occupation of waitressing. Out of the mouths of waitresses come some of the best lines ever spoken. An advantage of eating out solo is that you get to know them, and in my case, write down and collect their sayings. They are the unrivaled masters of not being victims.

Take Carolyn, my favorite waitress at the Silver Skillet in Atlanta. This was her response to a man who had threatened her:

"Let me tell you somethin'. You might think you're a big cig-ar, but I'll light you up and smoke you down anytime I want."

I almost feel sorry for the obscene phone caller who attempted to harass her once. When she answered the phone, he launched into a lurid description of his "anatomy." Carolyn let him finish his sentence before shooting back, "Well, bring that little thing on over, and let's see how it likes nuzzling the barrel of my .45." The next thing she heard was a dial tone.

The Way of the Cracker Queen is not a flaky, feelgood response to life. It's full-throttle whup-ass: unleashed and unapologetic. This ain't no sing-along, girls and boys. This is a war cry.

Outlaw Virtues

You were once wild here. Don't let them tame you.

—Isadora Duncan

Five out of five Cracker Queens agree:

BLIND OBEDIENCE TO THE LAW IS JUST PLAIN UNBECOMING.

The "law" refers to any authority figure—whether banker, bill collector, preacher, landlord, spouse, parent, taxman, repo man, police officer, or any other representative of local, state, or national government.

When you grow up in the margins, the law is your enemy and not something you want to be associated with. It's what can remove you from your home, haul your daddy off to jail, and take away your dog. It's always intruding or looming, trying to insert itself into your business. So we learn how to evade it, trick it, and stay under its radar as long as possible.

But since Cracker Queens are not always right or upright, we inevitably end up in fisticuffs followed shortly thereafter by handcuffs. When this happens, we never kowtow. To do so would be to break the Code of the Outlaw. That's why Cracker males consistently show their asses in front of the cops. They know there is no bigger turnoff than a man who cowers before the law.

One of our favorite pastimes is messin' with the government. We scheme and scam the feds with the agility of a *Fortune* 500 CEO. Me-Maw never worked a day in her life and didn't need to. She'd figured out how to exploit every government program created: food stamps, Medicaid, Social Security, utility assistance, public housing, surplus cheese, you name it. She enjoyed a comfortable life and had enough left over to sponsor Little League teams and a drag racer. She also parlayed some of those government checks into seed money to fund a highly lucrative business as a loan shark. Me-Maw extended seven-day loans at a minimum interest rate of 100 percent.

When I was an impoverished college student, I engaged in a bit of skullduggery myself. I was in arrears with the phone company and couldn't get a phone line until I paid the outstanding bill. So I called them and posed as an Indian graduate student named Ringa Dingh. I made her an Indian because I could do the accent—and because she wouldn't need to give them a Social Security number. The phone company was happy to set up an account for her. I chatted away on Ringa's line until they disconnected her for nonpayment too.

I thought I was so slick—until something suspicious appeared on my credit report eleven years later. In the process of buying my first home, I could not be approved for the mortgage loan until that mysterious debt was resolved. It said that I owed the phone company $700. This didn't make sense because I had long since paid my old debts. It turns out that a former college roommate had gotten a phone line by using my name and Social Security number. As I was telling her about my Ringa Dingh ruse, she took the idea and ran with it—all over me.

I didn't fight the charge; I settled it because I acknowledged it for what it was: not an injustice but a karmic comeuppance. Nonetheless, I'm still rather proud of coming up with a name like Ringa Dingh.

Clearly, Cracker Queens are not always on the side of the angels. Blues legend Robert Johnson wasn't in Iowa when he sold his soul to the Devil—he was in the dirty, beguiling South, same as us. Like him, we believe that a bit of vice, indulgence, and rule-breaking nourishes the soul.

I must admit that I'm sad when bank robbers are caught (assuming they didn't hurt anyone). I get mad when code enforcers make someone remove rusty cars and appliances from their front yard—or make an old hippie cut his four-foot-high grass. Perfect lawns and obsessive neatness are overrated. Life is wild and untidy, so why fight it?

A delicious satisfaction comes from seeing people break stupid laws. It shows that a healthy defiance is still circulating in a mostly cookie-cutter culture. Whatever happens, do not let them tame you.

Majestic Distinctions

Moving Forward

> The aim of life is to live and to live means to be
> aware, joyously, drunkenly, serenely, divinely aware.
>
> —Henry Miller

Look around you. What do you see? People who are
stuck. Friends, family, and coworkers who won't move
forward. They wallow in the same state of mind for
years, perhaps their whole lives. This mind-set robs them
of the good stuff, perpetuates "bad luck," and keeps them
from the banquet I keep harping about.

Most folks who live in a rut don't even know it, at
least not on the level of perception that I want to talk
about next: walking in awareness.

Walking in awareness means that you are living
consciously—aware of yourself, open to others, wide-
awake. This consciousness allows you to listen to the
hearts of others because you are not self-absorbed like
the Rutdwellers. Since you really hear the people around
you, you can focus on their needs and on how to show

them love and kindness. As you practice this act of giving, you learn more about yourself and develop in the process. And when the center of the Universe shifts from you, you become much more smart, beautiful, and fabulous. Since the Rutdwellers care only about themselves, they remain stalled, stunted, and stagnant.

Rutdwellers are the dregs, the residue that settles at the murky bottom. They cannot see clearly because their perspectives are clouded by selfishness and self-victimization. Many Cracker Queens begin life among the dregs of society, but we rise above the worst elements of our upbringing while still embracing what we are. This causes transparency to appear in the murky places.

When the tide is breaking at our feet, we Queens know it's time to make a change and move on. The Rutdwellers view the tide as just another slap in the face. To them the water resembles backwash in a beer bottle; it has no value. But we greet it with respect and appreciate its warning. The Rutdwellers would no doubt commiserate with Oscar Wilde that, "Life is one part lullaby, two parts fear." They are quite right, but only if you choose it to be so.

Beware of Cheap Imitations

In the interest of public safety, the following is presented as a Public Service Announcement:

Rutdwellers masquerading as Cracker Queens have

been spotted in your town. Do not be fooled. These loud creatures travel in swarms and parade about noisily. In reality, they are just boldly going nowhere. Maintain a safe distance from these shallow wannabes: They are lemmings and wussies dressed in Queenly attire. Take measures to avoid them.

Be advised that should you aspire to Queendom, you cannot attain it by adopting only the surface elements and ignoring the core values of love, forgiveness, and gratitude. It's fun to cackle and carry on, but it will not get you to the throne. I repeat: it will not get you to the throne.

Give Up, Hell!

When I was a little kid, Evel Knievel was a megastar: the world's greatest daredevil. He thrilled us with motorcycle stunts that often ended in bone-crushing crashes. His failures were a great part of his appeal, because everybody loves a good accident, and more important—he never gave up.

A friend had an Evel Knievel action figure that came with a motorcycle and ramp designed to reproduce his trademark collisions. I'd rev up the bike, let him go, and we'd hold our breath as he went airborne off the ramp. And just like the real Evel, he'd be ready to do it again and again and again.

Once I got a bit older I remember getting the impression that Evel was pretty smarmy, but I was still glued to the TV whenever he'd attempt to jump over a line of double-decker buses—or a canyon.

As a fragile old man, he described himself as "nothing but scar tissue and surgical steel." When he said that, I realized that he was a true Cracker Queen. Scarred but resilient. Feisty, tenacious, and attracted to trouble. Prone to wearing spangled jumpsuits.

After his death I enjoyed reading the obituaries. They brought back vivid memories of his ill-advised exploits both on the ramp and off. But one line in particular stopped me in my tracks: "It seemed he could not think of things big enough to jump over."

Whoa.

There is much of the Queen in that statement—taking a gamble despite huge risk . . . getting injured but still scratching and clawing your way out of the pit . . . Never, ever giving up.

I should note that giving up and quitting are not the same. Giving up is to surrender while knowing when to quit is essential to one's happiness. When your joy is gone, you know you've made a wrong turn. Evel found bliss when he soared off the ramp, but when you find yourself in unhappy freefall, it's time to quit. Say goodbye and let it go. Something better is beckoning.

Resourcefulness

When the nuclear button is pushed, you want a Cracker Queen in your fallout shelter. If on the battlefield, you won't find a better warrior than a Queen. And if your car is broken down on the side of the road, pray that one of your passengers is a Queen.

Why? Because no one can touch the resourcefulness of a Cracker Queen. She'll pour her cocola on the battery terminal and get the car going again. She'll outsmart any foe because she has had so much practice with the government. And she will make the canned goods in the fallout shelter last twice as long. That's easy for someone who figured out how to feed four hungry mouths on less than three dollars a day.

Queens learn early that they have to be clever to survive. Generations of poverty instill a knack for getting by with less, doing more with little, and devising innovative solutions.

I've never forgotten a story a college roommate told me about his mother. Apparently she happened upon a deer in the road that had just been struck by a car and killed. Knowing that one deer provides ample amounts of meat, she hoisted him onto her pickup, dressed him, and prepared him for processing. The family had every venison dish imaginable that year. Twenty years later, and I'm still in awe of that woman.

Our resourcefulness comes from simple assumptions that may seem cynical but have served us well:

You cannot depend on or count on others.

Do not put any faith in people; they will let you down when you need them most.

It's best to do it yourself whenever possible; self-sufficiency is an exalted virtue.

As a result of these beliefs, we are consummate planners and organizers. Another rule we live by is to always have a backup.

Although we are typically hardworking, we're also crafty enough to avoid labor entirely. Me-Maw outwitted the system for fifty years. She created her own system to prevent being enslaved by another's. Some might call her Me-Maw the Moocher, but you can't argue with her success.

Nothing makes one more resourceful than being broke. When I was seventeen, I found myself in Paris, flat busted. I played my flute on street corners, but busking wasn't enough. Then I remembered a strategy used by 1970s supermodel Jerry Hall when she was young and traveling in Europe. Her ploy worked perfectly.

I would don a dress and perch in the lobbies of the finest Parisian hotels. Eventually a businessman, usually an Arab or a pasty Communist, would approach and ask me out. I would agree to meet him for supper at the hotel restaurant. I then refused to get in a car with him or leave the premises.

Those meals were exquisite. I gorged on course after course and pretended to find the men slightly interesting. As we were deciding on desserts, I'd excuse myself to go to the powder room or to place a phone call. But instead of doing those things, I'd mosey right on out of the hotel and back to my budget hostel, smiling wide the whole way. After a diet of stale bread, warm Pepsi, and pissy French attitudes, it was wonderful to get fresh foods and solicitous service.

When the incomparable Billie Holiday died, the hospital workers discovered that she'd taped fifteen fifty-dollar bills to her leg. Most tragic—and resourceful. Like Crazy Aunt Carrie, she could have been one of the greatest Queens ever known, but when the tide broke at her feet, she chose to be a Rutdweller. If you want to study rut behavior, look no further than an addict.

Mama has to be at the top of the heap when it comes to being resourceful. Consider how she finagled new school clothes for me each year from Kmart. Or how she increased her income by making crafts. She is the kind of person you want around when times are hard, a magician who can make something materialize out of thin air.

Insistent Knocks

Intuition has saved my life twice.

When I was at the University of Georgia, there was a period in which a knife-wielding rapist was prowling around town. I don't usually worry about such things, because it goes against my whole mastering-the-fear credo, but my gut kept telling me that I'd cross paths with him somehow.

On a Saturday morning I was awakened by an insistent knock at the door. All college students snooze until at least noon on Saturdays, so I thought that perhaps the person at the door had an emergency or needed help.

When the knock accelerated into a banging, I leaped out of bed and hurried to the door—actually I didn't make it all the way to the door because when I got about twelve inches away I slammed into an invisible steel wall. A quiet voice said, *"Open the door and you'll die."*

I stood there trembling, certain of the voice's message. The man kept banging—eventually I harnessed the courage to look through the peephole. I saw that he carried a brown paper bag in his left hand and wondered if the bag contained a knife. He knew I was on the other side of the door and leaned in close to the peephole. At this point I understood the true meaning of "losing my shit." Finally he turned away and headed down the stairs.

Hoping to get a better view of him, I ran to the room that faced the street and hid under the window. Then the eeriest of exchanges happened: At the exact moment that I peeked out the window, he stopped on the sidewalk and looked straight back at me. I didn't know it then, but he had also plunged a knife into the utility pole in front of the house before leaving.

But this cautionary tale doesn't end here.

A month or so later a dear friend invited me to a party at her place. Any other time I would have gone, but I became filled with overwhelming dread as she talked about how fun the event would be. Just to be nice I told her that I might come by, and she replied, "Ah, come on—even if it's just for an hour. . . . " But my inner guide had spoken loudly and said that I'd be in grave danger—or put into an early grave—if I went there.

By all accounts it was a jubilant gathering, so good that a number of partiers crashed there for the night.

After everyone fell stone asleep, a man with a knife crept into the condo and violently attacked my friend's roommate. She lost much blood from the knife wounds but eventually recovered. The assailant got away.

Was he the same man who pounded at my door? I believe so, even though I have no way to prove it. My instinct told me he was one and the same, and that's good enough for me.

These near misses showed me what could be at stake if I didn't listen to and trust my intuition. Cracker Queens do falter and bumble, but we do it less often than the general population. Because we nurture the innate gift that is intuition, we are spared a lot of grief. Intuition takes us directly to the answer, bypassing the usual rigmarole.

It may seem to onlookers that we make big life decisions without thinking. But thinking has its limitations— intuitive intelligence does not. Twice I've left secure, well-paying jobs for positions that paid significantly less and carried more risk. I'm sure that some thought I'd lost my mind. In a sense, they're correct. I silenced the noise of my mind so that I could hear what I needed to do. In each case, the new job brought fulfillment and led to amazing opportunities. Trusting my intuition required that I venture into the uncertain, and I was nervous. But it was OK, because I knew that intuition never errs.

There's no doubt that a Cracker Queen's constant and most reliable companion is her intuition. Unlike cheap hair dye or facelift-in-a-jar, it does not promise what it cannot deliver. It will not let you down. Queens have made the act of discernment an art form. This talent keeps us from squandering our fabulousness on the wrong people and situations.

Listening to your gut can be difficult business, and it takes diligent practice. Even the most seasoned intuitives have to work at it. In this case, the mind can be a terrible thing; it's the culprit that's always butting in, trying to push away intuition with worries, stress, pride, guilt, anxiety, shame, and false realities. Beware of "should-have" and "what-if" thinking. Keep a check on your ego. It's like a giant fear-manufacturing factory. Don't fall into that vat!

Sometimes we get bogged down in rationality and sophisticated reasoning. Instead of making the right decision, we opt for the rational and reasonable one. . . . At other times we overthink something to the point of chronic indecision.

It's common for us to reason, rationalize, and overthink because we're basing our decision on what the world will think about it. Or our mother, or husband, or best friend. When I lived in Savannah, I ended up in the emergency room with a nasty injury because I didn't want Jim to think I was a wimp.

Despite the fact that my gut was screaming at me, I shunned it and got whacked in the face in a freak accident. I put myself in harm's way because I was preoccupied with not appearing weak or unhelpful. It took a painful smack in the head to get me back on course.

Perhaps your instinct is telling you to go against prevailing notions, and it's making you uncomfortable. I understand, but you have to remember that people come to the table with their own set of limitations, biases, and agendas. They don't have what you possess: a knowingness of yourself that comes via an inner contact.

Let's face it, there are a lot of uninspired thinkers out there with equally uninspired advice and opinions for you. You can pretty much predict how they will respond to your intuitive decision-making. As you progress toward your higher purpose, you must not allow them to influence you. And why should you? You already have a trustworthy guide with you each step of the way.

Generosity

Actual phone conversation:

> *Me:* Mama, is something wrong?
> *Mama:* Well, I guess I'm a little down because a friend of mine stabbed and killed her boyfriend last night.
> *Me:* Oh, I'm sorry to hear that.
> *Mama:* Yeah, she's a real nice girl. We used to go

fishing together. I'm gonna have to find out where they're holding her so that I can take her a carton of cigarettes.

A man has been murdered, and Mama's top priority is to get cigarettes to the killer. Typical Cracker Queen behavior. Her generosity of spirit keeps her from passing judgment during a time of tragedy. Instead, she focuses on what she can do to help her friend. And she knows exactly what kind of gift will be most appreciated, considering the situation.

Cracker Queens are ingenious givers. We share what we have and sometimes give away more than we should. Because we're aware of our own flaws, we're always generous toward the faults of others. Occasionally we'll get duped into helping someone who is just using us, but it's worth the risk. Those who pimp us do not dissuade us from our mission.

Queendom also demands that we be generous without regard to getting anything back, including gratitude. This has been a pesky one for me because I place such stock in being grateful. For the longest time I'd get upset when my generosity went unacknowledged. Eventually I realized that my business is to work on myself and not anybody else. True generosity does not seek any acknowledgment. In fact, the less anyone knows about your munificence the better.

The neat thing about giving is that it really does come back tenfold. It's no accident that the most materially rich woman I know is also the most generous. Regardless of a Cracker Queen's net worth, we give lavishly of whatever we have. Whether it's the tube top off our backs or our last can of Pabst Blue Ribbon, it's yours if you need it. Just as important, we practice that rarest form of generosity: listening. We give you our attention and genuine concern. And even if you commit a crime so heinous that Bill Kurtis will one day talk about it on TV, you'll still have a loyal friend who'll show up during visiting hours armed with a carton of Newports.

One of the things I love about Mama is that she doesn't ask questions when someone is in a god-awful mess; she just renders aid. She has no hang-ups or second thoughts about whether the person is worthy. She knows that's not her affair.

A dear friend of mine was in a serious tight spot once and needed funds. I called Mama and "invited" her to make a contribution to this woman she'd never even heard of before. Without missing a beat, Mama told me to be on the lookout for a package in the mail. When it arrived I was to deliver it to my friend and watch her open it. She said nothing more.

Two days later I rushed the package over to my friend's house and excitedly presented it. She unpeeled the brown paper wrapping to reveal a shoe box. That's odd, we thought. Then she removed the lid to discover a tiny gift bag gleaming from the middle of the box like Kryptonite. I thought she was going to faint when she saw what was inside the bag: five hundred-dollar bills. It was just what she needed to solve her pressing financial problem.

Suddenly I found myself blubbering like a baby, bombarded by mental images of Mama as a child—barefoot, picking cotton under a full moon, going to bed sick and hungry, wearing threadbare hand-me-downs. My friend and I were overwhelmed by her generosity. Five hundred dollars is a small fortune for someone like Mama.

Or maybe I should rephrase that: at four foot eleven, perhaps Mama is the small fortune.

What Becomes a Cracker Queen Most

Pleasure

Southerners love their food with an ecstatic fervor. It's not uncommon for us to spend entire dinners discussing nothing but the meal in front of us. Here's a typical dialogue:

> *Diner 1:* Paw-Paw, see if that hoecake right there doesn't make your tongue wanna slap your brains out!
>
> *Diner 2:* Ooh, Bubba, you are not lying about that! There should be a law against somethin' tastin' that good!
>
> *Diner 3:* You ain't kiddin', but have y'all sopped up some of that pot likker with that hoecake yet? Now *that's* good eatin'.
>
> *Diner 1:* I don't believe there's a better meal to be found than the one right here in front of us. Not even at that new restaurant, the All-You-Can-Stuff Silver Trough Buffet.
>
> *Diner 2:* You got that right!

Diner 3: Remember how Granny, rest her sweet soul, would set out under that pecan tree out there and shell beans for hours and hours— and her with the Arthur-itis and all. . . .

Diner 1: Sure do, and I don't mean any disrespect to Granny and her sweet, gnarled-up hands, but I do believe these limas are every bit as good as hers. Shug, would you pass the chow-chow please?

Our cuisine is revered and enjoyed with such gusto that we take photos of our special meals so that we can relive them forever. Every Christmas I snap shots of the meal on the table. My photo albums have people in them too, but the meal is the main attraction. I have admired close-ups of hams and pear salads for years.

Taking pleasure in something as simple as a plate of black-eyed peas and collard greens means there's something to relish every day. Don't ever try to come between a Southerner and her culinary enjoyments. Likewise, don't dare separate a Cracker Queen from her pleasures.

Queens have a marked capacity for savoring everyday experiences. Being grateful makes us more attuned to the goodness of things. When it's received in gratitude, the goodness itself is more vibrant: It pops like a movie going from black and white to 3-D.

Just look at Queen Paula Deen, the sunny Southern cooking sensation from Savannah. She exudes delight, gratefulness, and a down-home wit. We all smile when she decides to toss in that additional stick of butter. Revel in it while you can. Cholesterol be damned!

We don't chase pleasure, but we expect to find it everywhere, even in the darkest moments. You may recall that when I was a kid Mama smashed out all the glass in Daddy's Pontiac. When I asked her about it thirty years later, she waxed nostalgic about how wonderful it felt to deliver each blow. Huh? In fact, she said each subsequent swing of the mallet was better than the previous one. When the mallet shattered, she used her hands and was tickled pink with finishing the job that way.

She was also quick to remind me that she was simply following through on a promise she'd made: She told him that if he didn't stay at home that night, she'd injure his car. "It felt damn good. He deserved every bit of it."

Cracker Queens are also noted for their love of fire, specifically burning things. When a no-count man has crossed the line, nothing satisfies more than setting fire to his clothing in the driveway. As soon as he sees those flames, along with the look blazing in your eyes, he will not be a problem again. Just as smoke drives out vermin, fire cleanses and banishes the rat finks in your life. And it's so purging and gratifying to strike the match and watch his most prized threads melt into goop, especially that limited edition NASCAR jacket you always hated. (Note: If it's not feasible to construct an outdoor pyre, select a small symbolic item and ignite inside.)

I once had a disgusting roommate who refused to

move out. Finally I had had enough and started dropping his possessions, one by one, out of the second-floor window. His pride and joy was an expensive vintage guitar. When I saw him walk up in the yard, I dangled the instrument out the window. He begged and pleaded with me to spare his precious guitar. Wading among the clothes and personal items I'd pitched below, he kept his arms outstretched in case I let the baby fall.

We brokered a deal: His guitar would be unharmed if he agreed to leave within the hour and never return. I sequestered the hostage in my room until he had cleared out. What an intoxicating pleasure to hand him the guitar through his car window and watch the taillights in the distance. I was never bothered by him again.

Play

> The worst thing about some men is that when they are not drunk they are sober.
>
> —WILLIAM BUTLER YEATS

When your tank is near empty, get playing—whatever your idea of play might be. Cracker Queens can put any kid to shame when it comes to having a ball. We're childlike but not childish. We know that playfulness is a form of sacred fun. The Universe loves it when we play. And it does not punish us if the play turns irreverent, so don't strap rules onto something that should be free.

Let loose—especially when you've been too serious

and sober for too long. Play is the ultimate detox for the day-to-day detritus we accumulate.

Solitude

Like many other women, I have a bad habit of overextending myself. I have lots of different interests and tend to take on too many projects. Sound familiar?

When I was in my twenties and early thirties, I'd keep pushing until I burned out. I'd get so sick that I'd have to miss a day from work. My body and mind would slam the brakes on and force me to rest. Or as Mama described it, "When Retta gets to that point, she just folds up like a billfold."

But not anymore. Now I catch myself when I start to feel fried, and I go to my writing shed for a dose of solitude. That shed is twelve square feet of heaven. Regular time by yourself is essential. Quiet contemplation reconnects you to who you are and builds up your physical, emotional, and spiritual reserves. It allows your intuition to show itself more clearly.

The closer you get to your authentic self, the more your enjoyment of solitude grows. If you can't handle solitude, something is fundamentally wrong. You'd better get to work on identifying the problem. Being uncomfortable with your own company signals that you've strayed from your genuine self. Solitude helps us to know ourselves and better manage and balance our energy. To be a Queen you have to be comfortable in your own skin.

Recite After Me . . .

As you endeavor to make the life of your dreams, frequent recitation of the Cracker Queen motto will help you focus and eventually triumph.

Recite after me:

LOUD

HARD

DEATH

Once more:

LOUD

HARD

DEATH![1]

Not everyone needs to know what those words stand for. In fact, if the right people overhear you reciting them, it might scare 'em off and save you a whole box of matches.

True Beauty Queens

Soon after I graduated from college, I was invited to judge a beauty pageant for African American teens. There were several gorgeous contestants, many average ones, and one who no one would put a bet on. I'll call her Karla.

1 Live out loud, laugh hard, and love life to death.

She was at least fifty pounds overweight and didn't have any of the physical sparkle we were told to look for. As I studied her flaws, she became more and more beautiful. I imagined the guts it took for her to enter the pageant and then turn its notion of attractiveness upside down. She was a fellow rebel. I loved her confidence and spunk—and total absence of sparkle.

The first time she swished her jiggly hips across the stage, the other judges gave her condescending smiles and looked at one another, their eyes saying, "Bless her fat heart. . . . Pitiful. . . . Not a contender."

Right then and there I set out to put Karla on top. She had an ace in the hole that no one suspected: a judge in her right hip pocket. I proceeded to award her perfect or near-perfect scores in every category: casual wear, talent, oratory, and formal wear. My exorbitant scores skewed the contest and vaulted her to First Runner Up. Everyone was baffled. How could the ugliest girl nearly steal the pageant title? By having the kind of beauty that counts far more.

You see, Cracker Queens find value where others see none. And while we appreciate physical beauty, it doesn't impress or concern us like the inner kind. A chipped teacup interests me more than an unblemished one. It has a story and a new beauty as a result of what it's been through. Queens recognize that beauty lies in the broken and imperfect. The teacup still holds water, after all. It's nicked but not out of commission. We can relate to that.

Most of us have obsessed over our looks at some point, but eventually we realize that our body is just the form we inhabit. It's a vessel, not a temple. It is built not to last. Guaranteed to deteriorate and decay. Flesh and bones matter not. You have to let them do what they will and be at peace with it.

A sense of humor helps. One day Crazy Aunt Carrie was talking about how her bosom was drooping as she got older. Instead of going under a plastic surgeon's knife, she chose to make light of it with a remark that made me slide off Me-Maw's sofa in laughter.

"Retta, I wanna tell you somethin'. My boobs sag down so low, I can flip 'em over my back and burp 'em! Sure can!"

Even crazy aunts aren't completely crazy.

Parting Words

Now we have come to the end. Or the beginning. Which shall it be?

I know that I've covered a lot of ground here, but let us get to the heart of the matter. When the excrement hits the oscillator, the most important thing to do is:

REMEMBER WHO YOU ARE—
YOU ARE A CRACKER QUEEN.

Acknowledgments

At times our own light goes out and is rekindled
by a spark from another person. Each of us has
cause to think with deep gratitude of those who
have lighted the flame within us.

—ALBERT SCHWEITZER

This book is a tiny offering to the great writers, musicians, and artists who have unfailingly rekindled the light within me.

First and foremost: William Butler Yeats, William Blake, and Leo Tolstoy.

Also, Gustav Holst, Cannonball Adderley, William Faulkner, Sister Marie Keyrouz, Pablo Neruda, Albert Schweitzer, Django Reinhardt, Langston Hughes, T. S. Eliot, George Jones and Tammy Wynette, Albrect Dürer, Martin Luther King Jr., George Bernard Shaw, Dylan Thomas, Vincent Van Gogh, Seán O'Casey, Hank Williams Sr., Hank III, El Greco, Ella Fitzgerald, Nusrat Fateh Ali Akbar Khan, Earl Hines, Ezra Pound, Otis Redding, C. G. Jung, Van Morrison, Yunus Emre, Lester Young, Seamus Heaney, Rumi and his translator Coleman Barks, and Paul Laurence Dunbar.

I'd like to thank my fantastic posse at Gotham Books: William Shinker, the publisher to end all publishers; Lauren Marino, the editor of my dreams and an extraordinary partner on this project; Erin Moore, my former editor and initial coconspirator; Beth Parker and Lisa Johnson, two publicity people who taught this PR person a thing or two; and Brianne Ramagosa, who never misses a beat.

Thanks also to Joanne Wyckoff, aka La Agent Suprema, who knew it the minute she heard it. If not for her, I'd still be daydreaming about this book over a grilled cheese at the Waffle House.

Many thanks to Donna Havrilla for arranging the introduction to Mr. Yeats in high school. To Susanna Capelouto, Sara Sarasohn, Judy Purdy, Sigrid Sanders, and Jim Morekis for early opportunities.

I am also eternally indebted to two folks in particular: Diana Morrison, the original inductee in the Cracker Queen Hall of Fame (that should tell you all you need to know), and Terry Hulsey, the artistic genius and my creative comrade from the beginning.

Thanks also to Shelly and Michael Miller for their spirited support; Shana Dezelle, the best colleague anyone could ask for; Judith Ann and Ron Witherspoon for showing me in my best light; Don Simmons for wise counsel; Jackie Crum-Slay for being the hostess with the mostess; Mary-Elaine Jenkins for toting her Cracker Queen poster from Washington, DC, to Edinburgh and points in between; Grace Fleming, for being a fine friend, writer, and all-around interesting specimen; Theresa Taoushiani for nourishment of several kinds; and the High Order of Whup-Ass Waitresses: Kathy Norton, Sheila Cleveland, Carolyn Graham, Casey Baker, Julie Hightower, and Kathy Tidmore.

I am grateful for the support of Terry Kay, Bob and Helen Strozier, Misty Hayes, Rafik Raphael, Kathy Bohannon, Alan and Anne Hall, Rosemary Daniell, Allison Webb, Gloria Hilderbrand, Diane Reese, Nancy Dorman-Hickson, Duke and Marcia Dufresne, Libby Leverett-Crew, and Joan Evans and that scrumptious tomato pie of hers.

A special appreciation goes to my colleagues at Atlanta Technical College: Audrena Howell, Sandy Barner, Lyn Farmer, Myrna Turner, Deborah Gresham, Fred Brown, John Correll, Harold E. Craig, Teresa Brown, Marilyn Smith-Robinson, Rodney Ellis, Alvetta Peterman Thomas, and most of all to the sparkly Joni L. Johnson Williams, a superb word girl in her own right. Thanks to the faculty, staff, and especially the students of Atlanta Tech.

I don't know what I would do without dear friends such as Melissa Powell, Gabe and Mae Loggins, René Garcia, Wendy Walker Way, Rachel Dugger, and Donna Boortz (who is also one spectacular mentor).

I prize the memory of Bob Burnett, Brenda Watts Jones, Martha Johnson, Ellie Hannon Judah, and my father—whose music plays on in each note I put on the page.

Thanks also to everyone who has come to a Cracker

Queen reading over the years or shared their stories with me. What a gift.

I thank my family for unending material as well as laughter through the hard times: Donna Byrd, Cecilia Graff, Dennis and Jacqueline Hannon, Susie Shepard, Irene Grace, Connie Johnson, Pat and Terry Hannon, Mel Judah, and an extra-loud shout-out to Dusty Jones. Words are paltry things when it comes to expressing the love I have for my mother, Sybil Hannon, the Queen of Queens, the woman who brought me into the world and can take me out anytime she pleases. This book is my love letter to her.

And then there are my soul brothers: Mitchell Bridgman and Robbi Kearns. They've been with me on the whole journey and enriched it beyond measure with their presence.

I thank Mitchell for adventures in Amsterdam that can't be talked about; for thoughtful insight and gallows humor; and for his kind, kind heart. What luck for me that you could not type.

I am so grateful to Robbi for listening and laughing; for piercing analysis; and for his lack of sentimentality. Not to mention gospel favorites on the autoharp, midnight pizzas, and much more that shall remain unspoken because we can't just up and get all gushy now, for God's sake. I'm glad you dropped the philosophy class.

Towering above all of these is that Juggernaut of Badness: my Jim—simply the best there has ever been or will ever be. I thank him For Every Thing.

Message to Book Clubs

I'd be delighted to talk with your book club over
the phone or in person. Please e-mail me at
contact@thecrackerqueen.com.

The Day of the Cracker Queen

By royal decree the first Saturday in May has been desig-
nated the annual Day of the Cracker Queen. Join us for
the festivities or find out how you can celebrate being
a whup-ass woman wherever you are. Get the details at
thecrackerqueen.com.